Tim

Time Well Spent
a practical guide to
daily devotions

Colin Webster

alpha

Copyright © 1999 Colin Webster

First published in 1999 by Alpha

05 04 03 02 01 00 99   7 6 5 4 3 2 1

Alpha is an imprint of Paternoster Publishing,
PO Box 300, Carlisle, Cumbria, CA3 0QS, UK
http://www.paternoster-publishing.com

British Library Cataloguing in Publication Data
A catalogue record for this book is available from the British Library

ISBN 1-89893-873-3

Unless otherwise stated, Scripture quotations are taken from the
HOLY BIBLE, NEW INTERNATIONAL VERSION
Copyright © 1973, 1978, 1984 by the International Bible Society.
Used by permission of Hodder & Stoughton Limited. All rights reserved.
'NIV' is a registered trademark of the International Bible Society
UK trademark number 1448790

Cover Design by Mainstream, Lancaster
Typeset by WestKey Ltd, Falmouth, Cornwall
Printed in Great Britain by
Caledonian International Book Manufacturing Ltd, Glasgow

'Not to us, O Lord, not to us but to your name be the glory, because of your love and faithfulness.'
Psalm 115:1

To my precious Vicki who sits on her step each morning and talks to her Saviour and friend. I love you with all my heart and dedicate this book to you.

Thanks to Ian who sent me my first set of Bible reading notes, which encouraged me to have a daily devotion in the first place.

Thanks also to R.T. Kendall at Westminster Chapel whose preaching inspired me to have a greater passion for the Lord.

Additional thanks to Peter Lewis, Matthew Evans and the members of Cornerstone Church in Nottingham who have helped and encouraged me to put this work into print.

I am grateful to Andrew Miles for all the artwork and to Chris Akhurst for his patient editing.

Contents

Foreword

My own Dad was a man of prayer. He would not think of going out into the day without thirty minutes on his knees. He now has Alzheimer's disease as I write this, having just reached his ninetieth birthday. I can still talk to him about the distant past, and I asked him not long ago: 'What made you want to pray so much?' He answered: his pastor Gene Philips. Gene Philips urged all his members to pray thirty minutes a day, and my Dad took this seriously.

This has rubbed off on me, and I urge the same for members of Westminster Chapel. Some have thought this over the top, but, I believe, there are a number who do it – and they are never sorry. We may have many regrets when we get to heaven as to how we spent our time, but we will never regret any time alone with God. Children spell 'love' T-I-M-E. I wonder if God regards our love in much the same way?

What is needed pre-eminently today is motivation. At the end of the day only the Holy Spirit can motivate us to want to spend more and more time alone with God. This book none the less should not only help motivate people to pray; it offers practical help –

which every Christian needs. The goal of a prayer life is that the Lord will descend to each of us and speak to us 'face to face, as a man speaks with his friend' (Exodus 33:11). This book puts that glorious possibility into everyone's reach.

I commend Colin Webster for writing this book. I have sweet memories of him when he was my own Assistant. He always seemed to know the right time to say, 'R.T., can I pray for you?' I can assure the reader, he is qualified to write on this subject. I pray that this book will have wide circulation. It will change many lives, and I believe the result could lead to a genuine outpouring of God's Spirit in many places.

R. T. Kendall

Preface

The brevity and simplicity of this book will inform the reader that this is not a scholarly work nor was it intended to be, for I am no theologian, nor, for that matter, a writer. This book is designed to be as practical to the reader as possible and it is with this purpose in mind that it has been written. I trust that whether you are a new Christian or a seasoned believer you will find the contents of help to your own devotional life, even if they just confirm that your time with God is in great shape.

The idea for this book stemmed from a seminar called 'Creative Quiet Times' which I led at a Cornerstone Church, Nottingham weekend in the summer of 1997. The notes from the seminar were then put into a pamphlet and made available to the congregation. I had no idea at that stage that one day those same notes would form the backbone to this book.

Some who read this book will be used to a set liturgy in worship and others to a freer style. That and other, similar factors make it difficult to determine how useful any one of the suggestions made in this book will be to the individual reader. You will all have to separate the wheat from the chaff for yourselves and only take on board the things that assist you personally in your walk with the Lord, although I ask you to be open-hearted enough not to ignore some of the challenges which the Holy Spirit may be urging you to consider.

If you are a new Christian I trust that this small book will both help you to see the need, and fuel the desire, to set aside quality time with the God of the Bible who would rather have sent his Son to die on the cross than live without you. May you enjoy and learn from every precious moment spent at the feet of your creator so that, by God's grace, you become more like Jesus here on earth, to the glory of the Father.

Colin Webster
Cornerstone Church, Nottingham. May 1998

Introduction

During my days at Moorlands Bible College in Bournemouth I used to beg a lift off a fellow student who had a car. He occasionally picked up one or two other students along the way, one of whom was a chap called John. After introducing myself to John I was somewhat taken aback when, after only a few moments, he asked me, 'How are your Quiet Times?' I don't know what you would have replied but I hesitantly said, 'OK, I suppose – as normal as anyone else's!' But to be honest, I was actually rather annoyed that he had asked me that question. Later on, however, I began to ask myself why I had been so annoyed by John's question. I think the answer is that 'Quiet Times' are so personal and private that we rarely, if ever, discuss them with anyone else. John's asking that question was like having someone enter my home uninvited and rummage through my personal belongings! The devotional life (or Quiet Time) of the believer is so private that we often don't know what other people's are like. For instance, do you know what your husband or wife's Quiet Time is like? What about your best friend in church – do you know

what their devotional life is like? The chances are that
the answer is 'No'!

It is with this in mind that I write down some glean-
ings from my own devotions and the devotions of
others in order to take the lid off this best-kept secret. I
also hope that you may have a fly-on-the-wall view of
other people's experiences. It is hoped that this insight
will then encourage you in your own personal devotional life with the God who calls us to walk with him
through this life and into the next.

1

First Things First

This book will not be like a magic wand that automatically sets you up with a great devotional life, without there being any work on your part. So, if you purchased it with that in mind, then already you will want your money back! I used to purchase books that had snappy titles, thinking that they would be a 'quick fix' to intimacy with the Almighty with little or no effort on my part. But I soon discovered that if things were going to be different with my walk with God then it was going to take time, effort and commitment.

In many ways those three words are being eroded by today's society. This is because we live in such an instant world, with instant coffee, instant communications, and instant results from our washing powder that we expect things done yesterday! Yet there is no product on the market which provides you with intimacy with God 'on the cheap', as it were! Even in the church you can't gain intimacy with the Lord by having the holiest of people laying their hands upon you – it just doesn't happen that way. If it did then the disciples would not have had to spend three years with Jesus getting to know him. If Jesus didn't allow his disciples any short cuts to intimacy with him, then we cannot expect it either. There are no magic wands or clever formulas. But, if you are willing to get to know the Lord better, I can assure you that he is more than willing to reveal himself to you.

If any relationship is to flourish and blossom rather than just survive, then it will take time, effort and commitment, and if this is true at the natural level in relationships between human beings, then it will be no different in our relationship with God.

Further, let us be honest with each other. We are dealing with a very private area of our lives which we all struggle with, so, right from the start we are all standing on level ground. I am not floating ten spiritual feet above you in this area – I stand alongside you as one who needs to hear this as much as anyone else.

Just to put you in the picture I have drawn a graph of the average Christian's Quiet Time cycle. Does it look familiar?

Our Quiet Times are full of ups and downs and occasions when they don't seem to be moving at all. That is perfectly normal. A quick glance at the Psalms will expose some of the spiritual ups and downs which even great men of God can suffer from.

Finally, there are exceptional circumstances that may mean that some of what I am saying needs to be applied in a slightly different way. If, for instance, you happen to be a busy mother or father with six screaming kids, you will need to apply things in the light of your particular circumstances. Likewise, if you have an unusually demanding time at work, the application of the material may have to be adjusted slightly. I personally have no experience of trying to sustain a strong devotional life whilst young children constantly demand my attention and so it would be foolish of me to offer advice on that score until such time as I am myself a parent. The chances are that by then I won't even have time to scratch my nose let alone scratch some comments on paper for you to read!

However, that doesn't mean to say that the circumstances of life should be used as an excuse for not having any devotional life. All that it ought to mean is this: you should still have a devotional life, but that devotional life may be different from other people's – (at least for a while). Indeed, this is the story of our lives for all of us: we all live in changing circumstances where very rarely does anything remain constant. Jobs change, our health may vary from day to day, our friends and family change too, and all of these factors need to be taken into consideration. The bottom line of Quiet Times is this. It will take effort, but it is worth the effort!

We must all strive to know God for ourselves, and not just rely on someone else's relationship and knowledge of God, such as our pastor's or our parents'. Instead, let us dig out a few gems from the mine of the Scriptures for ourselves, because I strongly believe that we will receive far more from our corporate times of worship on the Sunday if we have taken time over our private worship during the rest of the week.

2

What Is A Quiet Time?

The first time I ever heard the term 'Quiet Time' was from a young Zimbabwean called Simon Miller-kranko who was training as a hotel manager in London. The subject came up as we talked together one evening after church. Simon began to tell me something that the Lord had taught him through his 'Quiet Time'. I remember stopping him and asking, 'What's one of those?' Up until that point I had never known what to call the time of prayer and Bible reading which I had morning by morning. It had never had a name, rather as I had never known what to call that dangly thing which hung down from the back of my throat until I married a doctor (incidentally, it is called the uvula!).

Put simply, a 'Quiet Time' is time deliberately set aside in our day for seeking God. It is, if you like, an appointment. Indeed, it is the most important appointment of all, one in which we remove ourselves from the variety of people and things competing for our thoughts and concentrate on just one person with wholehearted attention, and that person is God.

It is called a Quiet Time because in order to have quality time we ourselves need to be quiet. That means switching off the TV or the radio, withdrawing by ourselves to a quiet place with our Bibles and spending time alone with God. It is something that extroverts may find rather more difficult than introverts, but it is essential none the less to draw ourselves away from every other competing voice.

Quiet Time questions

At this point in the book let me ask you some questions:
     Are you keeping a regular Quiet Time? If not, what is hindering you?

Are those hindrances avoidable or unavoidable?

Can you think of any reason why you shouldn't begin to have a Quiet Time from now on?

Do you think that in your busy life there are thirty minutes that could be sacrificed somewhere each day in order to spend some quality moments with God?

I would now like to give you some good reasons for setting aside time to be with God.

3

Eight Good Reasons For Having A Quiet Time

'To have a Quiet Time, or not to have a Quiet Time, that is the question,' but before you answer it I would like to suggest eight reasons for having a devotion.

i) to seek after God

Many years ago I gave a session on Quiet Times to the youth group at the church I then worked for. The young people were asked to share something of their own devotional experiences with the rest of the group (quite a brave thing for them to do!). One young man who hadn't been a Christian for all that long piped up and said: 'I have stopped trying to get *through* my Quiet Time and started to seek a meeting with God in my Quiet Time!' It was so simple a statement and yet I knew in my own heart of hearts that I was guilty of that very crime. We can be so interested in just getting through our set Bible reading or prayer list that we can kid ourselves that we have engaged with God, when all we have done is fulfilled our own Bible reading vows for that day. Yet the whole purpose of a Quiet Time is to meet with God and to have a real encounter with him. That is our priority and if we miss that then we have missed the whole point!

It was A.W. Tozer who said that 'contemporary Christians have been caught in the spurious logic that those who have found God, no longer need to seek Him'. Yet, as Stephen Eyre points out in his book *Time With God*, 'the paradox of the Christian faith is that those who know Him, **are** those who seek Him' (Eyre, p. 36). Pursuing God is something that the Christian, not just the seeker, must do, because, as King David once wrote:

> O God, you are my God, *earnestly I seek you; my soul thirsts for you, in a dry and weary land where there is no water* (Ps. 63:1).

David already knew the Lord at this point in his life, yet he still saw the need to seek after him! Any seeker who becomes a believer does not stop (or ought not to stop) seeking after God, for to do so is to stunt their spiritual growth.

This same truth is emphasized in Jesus' invitation to the crowds that gathered round him during the Feast of Tabernacles:

> On the last and greatest day of the Feast, Jesus stood and said in a loud voice, 'If anyone is thirsty, let him come to me and drink. Whoever believes in me, as the Scripture has said, streams of living water will flow from within him' (Jn. 7:37,38).

Unfortunately this verse loses some of its impact when it is translated into English, for what the Greek actually implies is this: 'If anyone is thirsty, let him *keep coming* to me and *keep drinking*!' (italics mine). It is a continuous action. So, in the same way that we need food and water on a daily basis, we need to seek God and have an encounter with him every day.

When that young man from my youth group came out with that statement of wanting to meet with God rather than just get through his Quiet Time I had to assess what needed to change in my own private devotions. At that particular time in my life I used to set myself a goal of reading a chapter a day from the Bible and then to praying for about half an hour. However, although I felt that my prayer time was a meaningful conversation with God, I found that my Bible reading had become just that, 'reading a book' rather than listening for the voice of the Lord speaking to me from it. Unconsciously I had made it my goal simply to get through a chapter and not to let God speak into my life from it.

When I realized this imbalance I decided, for a while anyway, to change my routine. What I ended up doing was this. Strategically, I chose to read one of the gospels so that I would visually (in writing at least) be encountering the person of Jesus. Then, I would read a few verses, or a paragraph at the most, from that gospel, chewing over each verse to glean, as it were, from every word the full impact of the scene in order to watch and listen to Christ in action. Within a short time I found myself engaging with the God of the Bible and asking him to help me to act in a similar way to Jesus. I had met with God once more.

Remember then that the whole purpose of a Quiet Time is not just to get through your reading or your prayer list, but to meet with God.

Quiet Time questions

Assess your own devotional style and ask yourself these questions.

Has your Quiet Time turned into a task that you just try to get through or is it an encounter with God?

Why might that be?

Is there anything that you need to change in your current Quiet Time structure that might bring freshness to it?

Let us move on to another reason why we ought to have a Quiet Time.

ii) because of our environment

Let us face it, there is very little in the outside world or in our workplace that naturally causes us to think about God! After all, how many of your work colleagues whistle 'Thine be the glory' as they sit at the office desk, or for that matter have a calendar of 'Golden Thoughts' pinned to their wall? The chances are that the answer is none! Our working world has a distinct absence of God. We need, therefore, to dwell on him in advance, prior to entering this godless desert.

Three thousand years ago King David recognized that the ancient world around him was full of idolatry and paganism. It was a world which neither affirmed

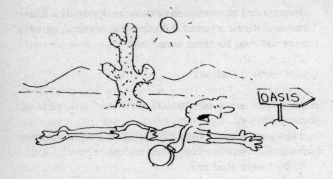

God nor stimulated a person to consider God. It was like a spiritual desert, hence he writes: 'O God, you are my God, earnestly I seek you; my soul thirsts for you, in a dry and weary land where there is no water' (Ps. 63:1).

If we cannot change our environment then we ourselves have to change in order to survive that environment. So, in the same way as a camel has to carry its own water supply because its natural environment is desert, we too have to fill our thoughts with God, drinking in as much of him as we can in order to sustain us throughout our working day.

Stephen Eyre points out the effect our society has upon us as believers. He says:

> In every aspect of society we are slowly institutionalising the absence of God. As Christians we lament this. But while we lament it we are being damaged by it. Like everyone else, we go through each day with little occasion to call upon God. Unless we take conscious precautions, we too slip into a pattern of spiritual darkness.

Despite our best intentions or even the depth of our convictions, we are affected. Like oxygen on metal, slowly, imperceptibly, the effect of our culture is to rust our souls (Eyre, p. 20).

Through our Quiet Time we create the necessary space in a busy secular world to allow the Spirit of God to break through. His word restores our thoughts, breathes reviving life into our weary hearts, and combats this rusting of our souls.

A.W. Tozer used to say that 'The Bible world is the real world'. Therefore, spending time submerged in the Bible and with the Lord is the thing that brings us into contact with reality and our true identity as children of God. It is through Scripture that we gain God's, and therefore our own, true perspective on life, family, work and ourselves. We learn afresh who we are and whose we are, which in turn helps us to behave in a God-honouring way.

iii) it is an incredible privilege

Unless we have an understanding of God's holiness, man's sinfulness and the Old Testament sacrificial system, we will never fully grasp the immense privilege which Christ's death and resurrection afford us. Yes, it is true to say that as Christians we have God as our Heavenly Father and that we can approach him at any time of the day or night wherever we happen to be. But we must never lose sight of the cost to God to purchase that privilege for us. Let me give you an illustration that might help you to grasp this.

Our sun is over ninety three million miles from the earth and yet the intensity of its heat is still felt despite that immense distance. It would be utterly inconceivable for us to imagine approaching that bright star for fear of being consumed by the ferocity of heat generated from its surface. In the same way that no human can even dream of approaching the sun without being consumed by its rays we too, by virtue of our inherent sinfulness, are unable to approach Almighty God because of his overwhelming holiness. Yet, the Son of God who is the Bright Morning Star has made the impossible possible. He has provided a way for us to do the inconceivable, namely to enter into God's holy presence despite the fact that we are sinners.

In the Old Testament times the temple, which dominated the city of Jerusalem, was the focal point for the worship of God. Every morning and evening the priests would sacrifice a sin offering there to atone for the sins of the people. The Israelites could then enter the inner courtyard of the temple, but it was only the priests who could offer up the sacrifices and enter the inner sanctuary known as the Holy Place. Yet even within that Holy Place was another inner room regarded as even more special, for situated at the far end of the Holy Place separated by a huge curtain which stood several feet tall was the Most Holy Place. This was originally the innermost sanctuary where the Ark of the Covenant rested. The only person who could ever enter the Most Holy Place was the high priest and he was only permitted to do so on one day in the whole year. That day was known as the Day of Atonement, when the sins of the whole nation of Israel would be atoned for by the sprinkling of blood from a sin offering (Ex. 30:10).

So revered was the Most Holy Place that the high priest used to have a cord tied round his ankle prior to entering so that, should he be struck down by God, the people would be able to pull his body out from the innermost sanctuary without endangering their own lives. Such was their awareness of God's holiness.

It is because of God's holy character that he cannot allow sinful people to approach him unless their sin is atoned for (Is. 6:3). Yet the wonder of the gospel is this: God himself was willing to pay the penalty for our sins in order that we the guilty ones can have fellowship with him. He did this by sending his son Jesus to die on the cross for our sins (Col. 1:21,22; Heb. 9:11–15; 1 Jn. 2:1,2). Someone once said that 'when we look at the cross we see that God is so much more angry with us than we had ever dared fear and yet is so much more merciful that we had ever dared hope!' It cost God everything to enable us to draw near to him so let us be sure to use the immense privilege that he purchased for us (Heb. 4:14–16; 10:19–22).

Quiet Time question

Are you taking full advantage of the privilege which Christ's death has purchased for you?

Why not thank God now that in his mercy he doesn't keep you at arm's length but allows you to draw near to him?

iv) it is a wonderful opportunity

I wonder how you view your Quiet Time? Do you sit
down with a slightly heavy heart as you open your
Bible rather as a student sits down to an obligatory
exam and with a sigh thinks, 'Oh well, here we go
again!'? If that describes your devotional experience at
the moment then I suggest that you pray for a more
positive attitude, for the enemy has robbed you of the
joyful expectation of meeting the God of the Bible,
who is full of surprises, fresh beginnings and new
opportunities!

Warren Wiersbe, speaking of Quiet Times, said;
'We don't do it because it's an obligation, but because
it's an opportunity!' (Wiersbe, p. 38). If our Quiet
Time is viewed as an obligation then it will be robbed
of any meaning and blessing, and will eventually
become a burden. Spending time with God ought to be
a delight and not a dread! After all, Moses did not
dread having to meet with God – he looked forward to
it. Indeed, Scripture tells us that 'The LORD would
speak to Moses face to face, as a man speaks with his
friend' (Ex. 33:11a)! I might dread meeting my
enemies but I look forward to meeting my friends.

It is incredible to think that Moses met with God as
his friend. I can't think of anyone more important in the
world who I would like to know as my friend than God!
Our relationship with Jesus is the most important relationship we enter into. The people we spend the most
time with often influence our attitudes, and can even
mould our character. The same is true of time spent
with Jesus. Something of him rubs off on to us.

v) it pleases and honours God

My wife and I love walking and at every possible
opportunity we head out to the nearby Peak District to
enjoy a day hiking in the hills and scouring the coun-
tryside for good tea shops. As we walk we often talk
about our work, the Lord and each other: it is our time
to catch up on the week. Vicki works as an anaesthe-
tist in a local teaching hospital and on one of our
walks I just happened to ask her what she thought
about as she sat there in theatre. She paused for a
moment, then gave her response. Her reply really
moved me. She said, 'I think about you . . . in fact I
think about you all of the time!' Although that may
seem a bit gushy to you, what she said was very precious to me. Yet as I thought further about those
words I realized that that is *exactly* what God would
have replied if you or I were to ask him that same question. 'I think about YOU . . . I think about YOU ALL
THE TIME!' would be his reply.

Let me tell you that this is not wishful thinking, it is
true! You and I are always in the mind of God; he
never forgets us, not for one moment of one day. Proof
of this is found in the prophecy of Isaiah where God
speaks of his total devotion to his chosen people Israel
despite their rebellious ways: 'Can a mother forget the
baby at her breast and have no compassion on
the child she has borne? Though she may forget, I will
not forget you! See, I have engraved you on the palms
of my hands' (Is. 49:15,16a). What incredible words!

King David too realized this same truth three hun-
dred years before the prophecy of Isaiah when he

wrote: 'Though my father and mother forsake me, the LORD will receive me' (Ps. 27:10).

This verse is particularly important in our day and age when so many children are growing up in one-parent families. Children can be left with the feeling that they simply don't matter and unfairly blame themselves. If you feel like this or have been the victim of a broken home then you need to be reassured that even though your natural father or mother may forsake you, your Heavenly Father will never abandon you. You are always on God's mind because he loves you and enjoys your company. You have his word on it!

Have you ever thought about that before? God actually enjoys your company not because he gets lonely, but simply because he enjoys you: that is why he made you (Gen. 3:8). God enjoys our attention, our time, our sharing our very lives with him. So, even if you don't get through everything that you intended to read or pray about on any particular day, it doesn't matter to him. The thing that he appreciates, is that you have taken the time and trouble just to be with him – he delights in that. The Scriptures say that God sings over us (Zeph. 3:17) because we mean so much to him.

You don't have to approach him wondering if he is going to be in a good mood that day because, unlike us, God never has an off day, he never takes a mood swing, he is always just the same. He never sulks or holds a grudge against us, because he can forgive us more easily than we can forgive ourselves. Each morning we find him just the same as he was yesterday. His personality and character do not change; nor does his love for us change either, for God himself says, 'I have loved you with an everlasting love; I have drawn you with loving-kindness' (Jeremiah 31:3).

In view of this, the most honouring thing to do at the beginning of any day is to acknowledge that that day, and your very life in it, is the Lord's, and, more importantly, that he wants to walk through every moment with you. Each day, by spending a portion of our time alone with God, we are affirming what so few people in the world or in our workplace acknowledge, that God matters to us and we matter to him (Eph. 2:10; Col. 1:16 Heb. 1:3a). The psalmist captured a vision of this when he wrote: 'Know that the LORD is God. It is he who made us, and we are his; we are his people, the sheep of his pasture' (Psalm 100:3).

This very day acknowledge afresh that the Lord is God and recognize that you are the sheep of his pasture and he is your shepherd.

Quiet Time question

Have you given up having a Quiet Time because you
were not getting anything from it? If so, have you ever
thought that you might be denying God something,
namely the attention of one of his precious children?

vi) it affects us

Our devotional life means something to God, but it
also means something to *us* – we benefit from it! We
may not feel so at the time; indeed, on some occasions
our devotions may have seemed a waste of time as we
have apparently received nothing from it. Yet, even in
those seemingly dry moments God is still doing an
invisible work within us. If we are studying his word
and taking time to be with him then the promise will
come true that he will not allow his Word to return to
him empty (Is. 55:11). The time that we have spent
with God will have a *pay day*.

There are occasions when it appears to us that we
are receiving nothing from our Bible reading (there
may well be reasons for this which I will comment on
later). Yet, my own experience has proved that often a
situation or circumstance will crop up that very same
day about which the wisdom or insight of the word
read in the morning had something to say. On other
occasions I have found that a passage that seemed to
wash right over me without having any impact, actually helped me months later to understand another
passage of Scripture and that the meaning was

enhanced all the more by that apparently futile study weeks earlier.

The same can be said about prayer. I don't know if you have ever thought about it like this before, but at the end of your life you will never have cause to regret one single moment spent in prayer. You may regret other moments in your life, but those spent in prayer will have been the wisest investments of time that you have ever made, indeed, prayer is an investment waiting to pay out its dividends! Some of those dividends may never be known to you in this life but I assure you that they will be revealed to you in the next. Heaven will be full of answers to prayer. I am sure there will be people or situations that we only prayed about once and yet years later (in heaven perhaps) we will see that God really did hear . . . and answer us, just in the same way that the Lord answered Daniel even though Daniel thought that his prayers were being ignored (Dan. 10:10ff.).

the golden rule

Generally speaking, I have found this rule to apply: If I have a Quiet Time and don't get anything out of it, I still feel better than if I have not had a Quiet Time at all! Having a Quiet Time gives God an opportunity to speak to me. Not having a Quiet Time almost guarantees his silence! It is rather like trying to get through to a company on the phone. If you pick up the phone and call, you may be put on hold and you may not get through when you wanted to, but eventually, through persistence, you will get through. However, if you don't phone at all then you are guaranteed not to get through!

Quiet Time question

Have you given up having a Quiet Time because you didn't seem to get through to God, or because God didn't seem to get through to you?

How else do you think God can speak to you if you don't pick up the receiver (the Bible) and speak (prayer)?

vii) it affects others

A famous concert pianist was asked about the amount of practice required to retain his high standard of musicianship. The pianist said, 'If I stop practising for one day I notice it, if I stop practising for a week my friends notice it, and if I stop practising for a month my public notices it!'

I think that the same can be said of our Quiet Times. If we stop for one day we notice it and feel somewhat depleted. If we stop for a week or so then those closest to us begin to notice it, and after a few months – everyone can notice it!

We all need to bear in mind that our devotional life affects others as well as ourselves, even though we might not realize it at the time. For example, when Moses had been with the Lord on Mount Sinai he didn't know that his face was shining, but the people noticed it (Ex. 34:29f.)! When the priests offered incense and sacrifices to the Lord, those back home could smell the effect of their time in God's temple as the incense smoke clung to their clothes (Ps. 141:2). In a similar way our lives do show the difference to others, even though we ourselves might be completely unaware of it.

This was the case with a recent convert called John with whom I had been spending time. John was telling me that within a few days of becoming a Christian his wife and family had spotted the difference, and within a week those at his workplace were approaching him and wanting to know what had changed in his life. John himself was unaware that he came across to others in that way but there was no doubt in his mind that his encounter with Jesus was the reason behind it all. Christ had affected him and the afterglow of that was affecting others.

Similarly, our time alone with God will gradually and indiscernibly be changing our values, attitudes, ambitions, goals and morals. So, just as the society in which we live is slowly and imperceptibly causing a rusting of our souls, so too our Quiet Time with God is slowly, and at times, imperceptibly, polishing our souls, and things that are polished catch the eye of onlookers!

Quiet Time question

Have you ever thought that if you don't have a Quiet Time you might be depriving those around you of the benefit?

As a way of putting other people's interests before your own, consider spending time with the Lord in prayer at the beginning of your day and see if others notice the difference.

viii) God provides time to be still

I remember hearing the story of a missionary who was trying to reach a certain destination by a certain time. Some of the local natives were carrying his belongings and they set off at a rather fast pace. One morning, a few days into the journey, the natives refused to go any further. When the missionary asked them why they were not breaking up camp and moving out, they replied, 'We're waiting for our souls to catch up with our bodies!' This is the story of so many people's lives today: their souls simply can't keep up with the pace that they are setting their bodies.

Nowadays we seem to be living in a society where a person's value is dependent on what they achieve rather than who they are. As a result many are driving themselves to the very limits of endurance in order to spend a few more hours at the office to finish the project, impress the boss, or receive the promotion. All the time I am meeting people who are just worn out, too tired to enjoy their work any more. They are not living; they are just surviving! What is lacking in people's lives today is a day of rest!

The Lord himself saw the importance of setting aside time for his people to rest and be in his presence, to the extent that he programmed into our weekly schedule a day of relaxation and reflection which he called the sabbath (Ex. 20:8).

> 'Remember the Sabbath day by keeping it holy. Six days you shall labour and do all your work, but the seventh day is a Sabbath to the LORD your God. On it you shall not do any work, neither you, nor your son or daughter, nor your manservant or maidservant, nor your animals, nor the alien within your gates. For in six days the LORD made the heavens and the earth, the sea, and all that is in them, but he rested on the seventh day. Therefore the LORD blessed the Sabbath day and made it holy.'
> (Exodus 20:8–11)

Amongst other things the sabbath was to be kept holy and separate as a day for focusing on God. But in addition it was to be a day that would break us away from our usual toil and routine of life and give our bodies some time to catch up. Indeed, the word 'sabbath' means 'to cease, or stop'.

As one preacher has put it: 'God doesn't want us to be workaholics any more than he wants us to be alcoholics!' You see, God isn't just interested in our spiritual well-being; he is interested in our physical well-being too. That is probably because he knows that the one affects the other. We matter to him more than our work! If we are too busy to pray then we are too busy!

God has seen the importance of setting aside time for us to be with him, and Jesus saw the necessity of drawing away from the crowd in order to spend time with his Father despite the demands and obvious needs that lay before him. Yet Jesus also recognized that God made the human body for his purposes and Jesus was not going to abuse the short life that he lived in the body whilst here on earth (Mt. 14:23; Mk. 1:35; 6:31–32; Lk. 6:12). So, if God saw the importance of time alone in his presence by creating space in the week and Jesus, with his tight 'schedule', saw the importance too, then we ought to see it as important!

4

How Do You Do It?

As a young boy I used to be fascinated by tricks performed by magicians on television. One of the commonest catch-phrases used prior to any trick's being performed was 'Abracadabra!'. In my naïvety it seemed that success or failure depended entirely on that one phrase.

If there were an equivalent sequence of words that could be said to enable us to have a successful devotional life then the nearest I think would be those that the writer and preacher Warren Wiersbe suggests; they are 'habit and system'. Naturally, saying these words won't make any difference to your devotions but the outworking of them I believe will! Let us consider these two words.

i) get into the habit

I had a habit which I was never fully aware of until I got married. My particular habit was to leave pieces of paper such as letters and magazines on any surface area I could find (perhaps you too have a filing system like this!). My wife would ignore the build-up of debris until it reached a certain height and then speak out: 'Colin, I wish you would keep this house tidy!' It was only after she snapped that I became aware of my tendency. Since then I have made a conscious (though sometimes unsuccessful) effort to file things in the proper way. To my surprise I can actually find things a lot more quickly now than with my old 'system'. I can assure you that my parents never taught me how to be untidy; it was simply a habit which I got into over the years.

The Oxford English Dictionary defines habit as being: 'a settled or regular tendency or practice' or 'a practice that is hard to give up' (*COD*, p. 529).

I particularly like the second of these definitions because if our devotional life has become something that is hard to give up then it will have developed into something that we simply can't live without. The presence of God is something that you and I can't live without!

Some people equate the word 'habit' with legalism, which is not a fair term to use. After all, we don't use 'legalism' for other things that we do regularly, such as eating our breakfast, cleaning our teeth or having a bath. Instead, these things are viewed as normal living. It is true to say that we can get into good habits or bad habits, but habits don't just happen overnight – they develop! That is why there are no magic wands for making Quiet Times happen.

Getting into the habit of doing something actually helps you to do that very thing with greater ease; indeed, Warren Wiersbe believes that 90 per cent of the battle of having a Quiet Time is won by getting into the habit. However, because we live in such an instant world where we want everything to happen now and not over a period of time, we may need some assistance in breaking ourselves into this habit.

'How on earth do you do that?' you may well ask, especially if, as you read this book, you don't even have any regular devotional time at all. Well, let me suggest to you this. Purchase a set of Bible reading notes which have a planned structure to them and a set portion of Scripture and prayer for each day. That is how I began to have a regular time with God. The reason that this helped me was that the reading was already laid out before me so I didn't have to play 'lucky dip' and waste precious time thumbing for a blessed thought for the day. It gave me direction in my reading. In addition, the notes that I used followed the calendar month, so I had a further psychological incentive for not missing a day, rather as some drug companies produce their medicines in easy-to-use 'one a day' pouches with the day of the week printed on each tablet.

Why not purchase some Bible reading notes and break yourself into the good habit of a regular devotional time? The habit will soon become such that you can't do without communion with the Father. Make your Quiet Time such that it becomes a part of normal everyday life like eating, sleeping, breathing or walking.

ii) work out a system

As well as being creatures of habit, we also like our systems. We like our programmes and daily planners so that we can see what we are doing with our day. In the same way, our Quiet Time ought to be a planned time which has structure to it and not a haphazard time. It could well be that that structure changes from time to time because of certain circumstances, but it is always best to have an idea of where we are going and what we are doing. After all, God is a God of order, not of chaos!

Having a system is particularly important when it comes to reading the Bible. If we do not have a system, then the chances are that we will only consider looking at those passages that are of interest to us. I have met people who say, 'Oh, I don't believe in using any kind of system.' Yet, very few of them can honestly say that their time with God is better as a result. Some people who don't have a system for reading the

Bible end up playing a game of scriptural lucky dip! If you use that system then watch out: you may land on Matthew 27:5 where it says (speaking of Judas), 'then he went away and hanged himself'! Not the most edifying of verses to meditate upon through the day, is it?

We need to have a system for reading the whole of the Bible, and not just the parts we like. All of the Bible is useful to us, not just our favourite top ten verses. The Bible is the mind of God; it tells us how he thinks and what he thinks. It tells us how God deals with his people, how much he values them and how his people ought to behave. In the Scriptures we read about the character of God and his plan of salvation as well as fundamental doctrinal truths of the church. God encourages us to read all of his Word, and not just a few choice passages.

Consider these verses:

- Man does not live on bread alone, but on *every word* that comes from the mouth of God (Mt. 4:4). (italics mine)
- *All Scripture* is God-breathed and is useful for teaching, rebuking, correcting and training in righteousness, so that the man of God may be thoroughly equipped for every good work (2 Tim. 3:16). (italics mine)

One of my lecturers at college jokingly used to say, 'Turn to the book of Obadiah . . . you can find that in the CLEAN pages of your Bible!' He said this in jest because if you ever look at the most well-thumbed parts of a person's Bible you can tell whether or not they read their Old Testament or just stick to the New. Too many believers neglect their Old Testament, feeling that it can't be nearly as edifying or exciting as the New. Yet if the truth be known the early believers by and large only had the Old Testament, which they never viewed as 'old' at all, but simply referred to as 'the Scriptures' (Mat. 21:42; 22:29; Acts. 18:28; Rom. 15:4; 1 Cor. 15:3,4). God's voice and God's breath is found on every page that you turn in the Scriptures from Genesis right through to Revelation. Men died to preserve those Scriptures for us; we ought therefore to devote time and energy to considering every sacred word inspired by the Holy Spirit.

Quiet Time question

Have you read the whole of the Bible? If not then set yourself a goal of reading every verse over a four-year period.

Get your Bible a bit more soiled!

when do you do it and for how long?

Charles Price, principal of Capernwray Bible School recalls that as a Bible college student, he and some friends learned how a saintly preacher from the last century used to rise at four in the morning in order to spend three hours in prayer before beginning his day. Thinking that this was the formula for blessing, they decided to do the same. They agreed that the one extra thing they would include was a cup of strong black coffee! They then settled down on their knees and began to pray. Three hours later, they woke up: their coffee was cold and their knees were aching!

What was possible for their hero was unrealistic for them. So, if three hours is too long for the average person, how long should we spend in prayer? At Westminster Chapel, where I used to work, we were encouraged to spend thirty minutes a day in prayer and I personally think that that is a good goal to aim for. Set yourself a basic goal, because if you don't you will have nothing to aim for. Try to work out a sensible and realistic length of time for your reading and prayer time so that on a good day you will hit it. On a bad day you won't – but you will always know what your ideal time should be. The one thing that I do know is this, you will never really change the world if you are spending anything less than ten minutes a day in prayer. Ultimately the matter is between you and the Lord.

the factors of life

Our lives are like the seasons of the year; they are full of constant change. Our work, health and family life can be as unpredictable as the weather and these factors will 'for a season' affect our devotional lives.

Your work or family commitments may play a huge part in determining when you have your Quiet Time. For instance, those who work from nine to five may find it easier to have their devotions in the morning because their day fits more generally with the normal pattern of life around them. However, those who work night shifts may have their devotions at the beginning of their working day at six in the evening. A parent may have had their day completely thrown off balance by a restless child in the night, with the result that they may have to take time once the children have gone to school, or when their children are sleeping. All these factors need to be taken into consideration and it could well be that during your Christian lifetime your devotions may have to adapt to the circumstances of life and work that you find ourselves in at the time.

5

What Did Jesus Do? (Mk. 1:35–37)

Have you ever wondered what Jesus' Quiet Times were like? I know I have. Although we cannot be absolutely certain it may be possible for us to know something of Jesus' own devotional life from an account found in Mark's gospel. Even though it is only a brief glimpse into the life of our Lord, it could well be an indication of Christ's usual routine (see also Lk. 4:42; 5:16).

Look at Mark 1:35–37.

> Very early in the morning, while it was still dark, Jesus got up, left the house and went off to a solitary place, where he prayed. Simon and his companions went to look for him, and when they found him, they exclaimed: 'Everyone is looking for you!' Jesus replied, 'Let us go somewhere else – to the nearby villages – so that I can preach there also. That is why I have come.'

Here we see four things about the Quiet Time which Jesus had:

- *The time (v. 35):* it was early in the morning! And
  don't you just hate the first word in that verse, *very*!
  Yet it could well be that this was Jesus' usual routine
  because the prophet Isaiah wrote in the third of four
  'servant songs' concerning the Messiah: 'The Sovereign LORD has given me an instructed tongue, to
  know the word that sustains the weary. He wakens
  me morning by morning, wakens my ear to listen
  like one being taught' (Isaiah 50:4).

Luke in his gospel account speaks of another occasion
when Jesus rose early: 'At daybreak Jesus went out to
a solitary place' (Lk. 4:42). So it seems that morning
by morning, Jesus woke up and listened to his Heavenly Father, receiving his instructions, like one being
taught (Jn. 5:19; 6:38; 8:28). From this verse then we
see something of the priority which Jesus placed upon
his time with the Father. It was an important priority
appointment.

The great Scottish preacher from the nineteenth
century, Robert Murray McCheyne, once wrote the
following advice to a young student training for
the ministry: 'Above all, keep much in the presence of
God. Never see the face of man till you have seen His
face who is our life, our all' (Bonar, 1978, p. 29). That
is the essence of a private devotion: to seek the face of
God before we seek the face of anyone else. That was
exactly what Jesus did.

- *His mental condition (v. 35):* he was awake! He was
  fully dressed and had a sharp mind. He wasn't giving his Heavenly Father the fag end of his time and

energy. His mind was clear not cloudy. He was giving the best moments of his day to his Father.

One of the reasons some people don't get anything from their Quiet Time is simply that their minds are not capable of retaining anything because they are mentally tired. Have you ever found yourself at the end of a weary day slipping into bed, extending an arm to the bedside table, picking up your Bible and beginning your Quiet Time? And how many devotions of that sort have also ended up being eight hours long, interrupted only by the sound of the alarm clock as it wakes you up from a deep sleep! Do you get the point? Give God the best of everything in your life, even the sharpness of your mind.

- *The place (v. 35):* he went to a solitary place with few distractions. Jesus did his utmost to withdraw from anything that would compete with undisturbed fellowship with his Father. I appreciate that this might be difficult for some people but, as far as it is possible and for however short or long a time, try to get alone with the Lord.

Apparently, some Christians in Hong Kong are so keen to be as alone with God as one can be in that highly populated island, that they will even travel out to the airport just to sit in the lounge area where it is less crowded! That is incredible! I have also heard of one busy mother who had a unique way of letting her young children know that she required undisturbed time with God. She would sit down in a chair and pull her apron over her face and, in those moments (however brief they must have been), she prayed to the Lord. I guess this was her way of shutting out the world for a 'blessing break'. Eventually her children learned that no matter how much they screamed, when their mum had that apron over her head she was dead to the world and alive to her God and they were not to disturb her!

- *The reason (vv. 35,38):* to be alone with his Father, because he had a busy day ahead! Indeed, Jesus had been busy the night before too (*vv.* 32–34). No one had a more tight schedule than Jesus: he only had three years in which to complete all the divine appointments that his Father had arranged for him! Yet, despite the obvious needs of those around him and his time constraints, we still read that Jesus deliberately withdrew from the crowds (and his own disciples) in order to be alone with this Father. One could say that Jesus was praying prior to starting his 'nine to five' job, just like most of us! If Jesus needed to spend time with his Father every day despite his heavy schedule, then so do we.

6

What Elements Make Up A Quiet Time?

There are basically three elements that go into my Quiet Time:

i) preparation
ii) reading
iii) prayer

I have set these elements out in the chart overleaf, and will expand on each point.

i) preparation

We need to prepare our hearts and minds to meet with God because our minds are buzzing around with so many other things that could easily rob us of quality time with him. In this respect I have found two things helpful: finding a place where I can have my Quiet Time (this is my 'place of meeting') and then settling down for a few moments and reflecting on whose

Preparation	Find your special place; a chair, a room, a desk, or a hill. Read a hymn, sing a song, listen to a tape. Tell God briefly if there is anything troubling you that might hinder this time. Ask God to meet with you during these moments.
Reading	Read a portion of Scripture, meditate on it and digest it. Find out something about God's character, power or wisdom, or the lessons learnt from other people's lives. Consider what God is saying to you personally. Is there a promise or a verse that you can take with you through your day?
Prayer	Use your Bible reading as a basis for prayer. Use a prayer list for others and for yourself. Wait on the Lord to see if he brings any to mind, then pray for them. Remember to check up on that impulse by giving them a call later!

presence I am entering (this is 'preparing my heart'). Let us look at both of these things in detail.

the place of meeting

Throughout the Bible God's people have found special places to meet with him. Mount Sinai was where Moses received the Ten Commandments. It also happened to be the place where Elijah ran to when he was suffering from burn-out (1 Kgs. 19:8). Jacob found his

Bethel, the place where he had a powerful encounter with God in a dream (Gen. 28:18,19) and he returned to that same place later to build an altar to the Lord (Gen. 35:6,7). The Tabernacle was known as the 'tent of meeting' for the Israelites and it was there that 'the Lord would speak to Moses face to face, as a man speaks with his friend' (Ex. 33:11). No wonder Moses entered the tent of meeting day after day if he could have an encounter with God like that!

We too need to find our place of meeting. Our place of meeting might be a certain chair (that is what I use), or room or even a step on the stairs (that is what my wife uses). It may be in the garden, or on a park bench (weather permitting!) or in a library (if it is during your lunch time). It could even be at 8.30

a.m. at your office desk before everyone else gets in to
work. As far as possible, try to find a place which is
quiet, or at least far away from distractions. That
is what Jesus did (Mk. 1:35). It might have to be in
your own home with a set of earplugs if you have
noisy neighbours!

preparation of ourselves

Because we live such cluttered and demanding lives it
can take time for our minds to unwind from the
stresses of the day and for us to enter God's presence
ready and willing to hear from him. That is why I suggest that we don't just rush into God's presence but
take a few precious moments of preparation.

Mentally and verbally praise and honour God for
who he is, and for what he has done in your life. Perhaps it might be helpful for you to read a Psalm of
praise, even if it is just the first three or four verses to
get you started. Alternatively, you may like to read the
words of a favourite hymn or chorus, or even listen to
a praise tape just to focus your mind and to recognize
whose presence you are entering. All this might take
you two or three minutes, depending on how hectic
life has been for you and the time restraints that you
are under.

You may find that your mind is full of so many
things other than God that you find it hard to settle.
Perhaps you have a busy day ahead, or one of the children is being awkward, or you have just received
another bill.

My suggestion would be this: tell God about these
distractions, because to do so is to bring God into your

busy life. Even that is time with God! You might not think that a particularly honouring way of focusing your mind on the majesty of God, but, in bringing all such distractions to God, I have found that he is big enough to cope with them even if I am not! The problem may seem large to us, but when God is brought into the equation we find that he dwarfs the problem. Besides, it also reminds you that God is actually interested in the minutest details of our lives – even the things that prevent us from drawing near to him. God can even accept complaints as a means of drawing near to him – the Psalms are full of them (Ps. 10:1; 13:1–4; 61:1–2; 77:1–2).

Remember that God is right there with you. In Psalm 16:8 David wrote, 'I have set the Lord always before me. Because *he is at my right hand*, I shall not be shaken.' Dr R.T. Kendall once told me that he used to begin his Quiet Time by applying that very verse. He would 'set the Lord' beside him as though he were right there sitting next to him in the room, and then he would begin to talk to him in prayer.

ii) reading

preparing to hear from God

Ever since I heard a preacher say that because the Holy
Spirit inspired the Scriptures he is the one who can illuminate our minds to the word of God, I have always
begun my reading by briefly asking the Lord to help me
understand his word by the power of the Holy Spirit.

We must keep praying as we read and, as the Spirit
illuminates a verse or a word for us, we should pause
to reflect on it in prayer. Have you ever watched people panning for gold? They swirl round the earth and
water until they find the deposit of gold at the bottom.
In the same way we too must swirl round with prayer
the word of God until we find such a deposit – and it is
there for the finding!

George Müller, that great man of faith and prayer
who lived in the nineteenth century, wrote the
following in his diary about his devotional life:

My practice has been for the last ten years previously, as a
habitual thing, to give myself to prayer after having
dressed in the morning. Now, I saw the most important

thing I had to do was to give myself to the reading of the Word of God, and to meditation on it, that my heart be comforted, encouraged, warned, reproved, instructed, and thus by means of the Word of God . . . whilst meditating on it, my heart might be brought into experiential communion with the Lord.

I began, therefore, to meditate on the New Testament from the beginning, early in the morning. The first thing I did, after having asked in a few words the Lord's blessing upon His Word, was to begin to meditate on the Word, searching as it were into every verse to get blessing out of it; not for the sake of preaching on what I had meditated on, but for the sake of obtaining food for my own soul.

The result I have found to be almost invariably this, that after a very few minutes my soul has been led to confession, thanksgiving, intercession, or supplication, so that though I did not, as it were, give myself to prayer, but to meditation, yet it turned almost immediately into prayer. When thus I have been for a while making confession, intercession or supplication, or having given thanks, I go on to the next words or verse, turning all as I go on, into prayer for myself or others, as the word may lead to it, but still continually keeping before me that food for my own soul is the object of my meditation. The result of this is that there is always a good deal of confession, intercession etc. mixed with my meditation, and that my inner man is invariably nourished and strengthened, and that by breakfast time, with rare exceptions, I am in a peaceful and happy state of heart (Steer, R., 1985).

From Müller's experience alone we can see the full potential and profit which arises from such a prayerful approach to the reading of Scripture.

b) read all of God's word (not in one sitting, of course!)

As I said earlier, don't play lucky dip with the Bible but work out a system whereby you end up reading all of the Bible over a period of a few years. This is important for several reasons.

Firstly, we need to become familiar with the whole word of God in order to get the whole message that God has for his people. If God inspired each book in the Bible and allowed it to be preserved for us, then it must be because he has something important to say which his people need to hear. The Bible is a part of the mind of God: it contains his opinions, his thoughts, his views, his desires. It speaks of his patient dealings with his people; it is full of Godly wisdom for this life and the next. It is precious. If we want to know what God thinks and how God thinks then we need to understand his word.

Secondly, reading all of God's word will save you much embarrassment in heaven! As the preacher Alec Buchanan used to say: 'Imagine how embarrassing it would be if someone tapped you on the shoulder in heaven and said, "Hello, I'm Habakkuk, did you enjoy my book?" Which would you rather have, a read Bible or a red face?'

c) how to read God's word

There are various ways to do your Bible reading. Some of these have already been mentioned, but here are some helpful tips.

read God's word in its original context!

It has been said that you can make the Bible say anything you want it to. That is true, but only if you read from the Bible out of context. We need to remember that each book in the Bible had something to say to its original readers and recipients. Therefore, we have to make sure that what we read is not something that the original writer did not intend. This is where commentaries come in handy. Although, one word of caution is necessary (especially to preachers): try not to turn your Quiet Time into an academic exercise or sermon preparation, or you may find yourself so engrossed in technicalities and word studies that you end up having no time for prayer.

read God's word as though God were speaking to you personally!

It doesn't really matter if you read a verse, chapter or paragraph a day; what is important is to know why you are reading it. The reason you are reading is to enable God to speak to you personally. He might be wanting you to know something about his character, or how you can live for his glory and avoid mistakes made by his people in the past. He may be giving you a promise that you can take to encourage you throughout the day. There have been many times when I have read a passage and seen a truth, an attitude, an action or a word that was relevant for something that was to happen that day. The Lord can, and does, use his word to equip you in advance for incidents that you are about to encounter.

Some portions of Scripture come alive to us in a more challenging way when we insert our own name.

For instance, what a challenge is presented to each of us if we put our names in place of the word 'love' in 1 Corinthians 13:4–7. Now that is something to live up to! And what about the pastoral letters of Paul? Imagine if they were written to you personally! Wouldn't you want to live up to all that Paul desired for your life? Here are a few passages to consider in this way: Jeremiah 31:3; Ephesians 1:3–23; James 1: 2–4.

memorizing Scripture

Memorizing Scripture is of immense benefit. It assists us in particular in the area of obedience. Psalm 119 has much to say about memorizing God's word:

> How can a young man keep his way pure? By living according to your word (v. 9).

> I have hidden your word in my heart that I might not sin against you (v. 11).

> Your word is a lamp to my feet and a light for my path (v. 105).

Clearly, memorizing Scripture is beneficial to the believer, yet how many verses of Scripture (other than John 3:16) do you know off by heart? Probably for many people the answer will be 'very few'! So let us try to rectify that with some tips on how to memorize Scripture.

Select a portion of Scripture, write it on a small piece of card and place it somewhere visible, such as by the bathroom mirror where you can look at it as you

are cleaning your teeth or shaving. Alternatively, place it in your bus pass and glance at it whilst standing in the bus queue or waiting for the lift (with some of the lifts I have waited for you could probably memorize a chapter!).

You will be amazed how many pockets of time in which we are thinking about nothing in particular we have in our lives; so why not utilize some of them by memorizing Scripture. My suggestion would be to spend a week on one verse. In that way in a year you could potentially learn 52 verses! Think about that!

I have to confess that I am not the most computer literate person in the world. In fact, when I upgraded the computer that had served me well for ten years I realized that I had moved from the stone age to the space age! But what I do know about computers is

this: you only get out of a computer what you put into it.

In the same way we only get out of our mind what we put into it. Jesus said to his disciples that the Holy Spirit will 'teach you all things and will *remind* you of everything I have said to you' (Jn. 14:26). But the Holy Spirit can only remind us of the things that we have taken the time and trouble to read and learn for ourselves! No one can lay hands on us at a meeting so that we become a walking concordance. Indeed, as a former pastor of mine used to say, 'If you were empty headed before you were filled with the Spirit, you will be empty headed afterwards!' If you and I want the Spirit to remind us of Scripture then we need to invest time in depositing Scripture into our memory banks so that he has something to fish out at the appropriate time.

Meditation

We memorize a passage in order to learn what it says to us, but meditate upon it in order to discover what it means for us. Meditation, unlike memorizing, involves taking a verse or passage and just chewing it over and over until we get the full flavour and richness of what that verse means. Small portions of Scripture are best for this.

Meditation is something which God encouraged his people to do:

> Do not let this Book of the Law depart from your mouth; *meditate* on it day and night, so that you may be careful to do everything written in it. Then you will be prosperous and successful (Josh. 1:8).

> But his delight is in the law of the Lord, and on his law he *meditates* day and night (Ps. 1:2).

> I have more insight than all my teachers, for I *meditate* on your statutes (Psalms 119:99).

Basil Pennington described the process of Bible meditation in this way:

> It is not a question of reading a paragraph, a page or a chapter. It is, rather, sitting down with a friend, the Lord, and letting Him speak to us. We listen. And if what He says in the first word or the first sentence strikes us, we stop and let it sink in. We relish it. We respond from our heart. We enjoy it to the full before we move on. There is no hurry. We are sitting with our friend . . . We let Him speak. We really listen (Eyre, p. 99).

Bible meditation is an unhurried saturation in the Word of God, it is a deep pondering on every word in a verse or passage, allowing each one to feed and influence the soul.

iii) prayer

Dr R.T. Kendall has called prayer, combined with Bible reading, 'the ABC of getting to know God'. To put it simply, prayer is talking with God.

a) remember prayer is work

Prayer has been described as 95 per cent perspiration and 5 per cent inspiration. It takes effort. It isn't like work, it is work! Paul said that Epaphras was 'always wrestling' in prayer for the Colossians (Col. 4:12). That word 'wrestling', or 'labouring' as the Authorized Version has it, is the same one used to describe the agonizing prayer of Jesus in the garden of Gethsemane.

There will be times when we pray about something and it will feel as though are in a wrestling match: this will be particularly true when we pray specifically for the lost. The Devil will do everything he can to discourage us from praying for the salvation of others, because we are on the offensive. But we should persevere, because, as one hymn writer has said, 'Satan trembles when he sees the weakest saint upon his knees.' Prayer is one of the most powerful weapons in the armoury of the Christian.

b) what do I say?

Don't worry about your language! You don't have to speak fluent 'Zionese' with all its 'thees' and 'thous'! Thankfully God looks at the heart and doesn't mind hearing short, simple prayers, as long as they are sincere. Indeed, that is what Jesus taught his disciples (Mt. 6:7). You might find it helpful to speak out audibly to the Lord, although he can hear us just as easily when we pray silently.

c) what do I pray about?

Pray about anything and everything: the family, business, friends, work, the world, church and you! If you are only praying for yourself, then make sure that you pray for others too. Often we can pray for no one else but ourselves because we feel in such deep need, but remember that other people have needs too. Praying for others helps us to take our thoughts off ourselves and to carry another person before the Lord. The apostle Paul is a perfect example of this, for he prayed for others even though he himself was in prison, in need of prayer (Eph. 1:15–23; 3:14–21; 2 Tim. 1:3–7).

d) one possible prayer structure

A pattern for prayer that you might like to use is **ACTS:**

Adoration, Confession, Thanksgiving, Supplication

Adoration

Worship and adore the Lord, thanking him for who
he is. You may like to use a psalm or a hymn to
assist you in reflecting upon what a great and
mighty God we serve. God loves to hear us affirm
his greatness, because establishing that in our own
minds assists us in our approach to him in prayer.
We ourselves then realize that there is no problem
too great or small for him to handle.

Confession

Bring to God the things that you know you need to
ask his forgiveness for. You may choose to confess
the sins that you are aware of out loud. Perhaps you
might want to use Psalm 32, 51, or 139 if it helps
you. John Calvin used to pray at the end of his

sermons, 'Lord help us to hate our sins enough to turn from them.'

Remember, always claim from God the cleansing power of the blood of Jesus that he promises and then leave your sin at the cross (1 Jn. 1:9). Don't spend all of your time wallowing in self-pity: Christ wants you to rise from a fallen state; he wants to lift up your head and instruct you in the way of righteousness. Ask the Holy Spirit to help you to resist or overcome any sin that seems to be besetting (1 Cor. 10:13).

Thanksgiving
Thank God for answers to prayer, and for his goodness and daily provision. This is where keeping a prayer list or journal comes in handy because there are so many answers to prayer that we often forget to acknowledge gratitude to the Lord.

Supplication
This is where we intercede for the needs of others. Bring to God the concerns for the day. These may include your family, yourself, missionaries or those in your fellowship who have particular needs. Remember too to pray about witnessing opportunities at home and at work, as this helps you to keep an eye out for such opportunities.

e) keep a prayer list

One of the things that I would encourage every Christian to do is to have a prayer list. You might want to list inside your Bible a number of people who you will pray for. Or, if you want to be more specific you might like to use prayer cards. Buy some index cards and divide them up like this:

Date	Request	Date	Answer

You can then put in specific prayer requests for your-self or others. It could be that you use one prayer card for your family, one for missionaries, one for those you are trying to witness to and one for yourself. You can use as many cards as you like!

Here is an example of how you might want to pray for a friend at work:

Date	Request	Date	Answer
4/2/98	Pray that I will make friends with the new person at work.	9/3/98	The new person is called John and we managed to have lunch together for the first time.
19/7/98	Pray that John will begin to ask questions about the Christian faith.	1/8/98	John has been asking me about the things we have seen on the news recently and this has led me to share something of my faith.
26/8/98	Pray that John will come to the gospel choir event in September.	25/9/98	John came along and enjoyed the night.
18/9/98	Pray that John will join a Discovering Christianity group.		

Some of my cards have very long-term prayer requests, so the chances are that the request side of those cards are not filled in as rapidly as others. None

the less, I find it helpful to have something to pray for.
For example, your personal prayer request list might
look something like this:

Date	Request	Date	Answer
	That I will become more patient.		
	That I would be less proud and not rob God of the glory.		
	That I would be bolder in my witness.		
	That I would see the best in people.		

Requests like these will probably not all be answered
until we get to Heaven, but at least if we pray about
such things we are reminding ourselves of what we
believe the Lord would love to deal with in our lives,
however long that process might take!

In order to develop such a personal prayer list I
sometimes find it helpful to think of what Jesus might
have written on his 'prayer list' about me. What would
he be praying for me right now? Think about that for a
moment for yourself: what would Christ be praying
for you? Why not write down some things on an index
card?

be missionary minded

I believe that every Christian ought to pray for at least one person on the mission field. Indeed if we are not thinking World Mission then we are not thinking the way God thinks (see Mt. 28:19,20). Personally, I find it helpful to have an index card with a missionary's photograph on one side and a copy of their prayer requests from their latest newsletter on the other. That way my prayers are specific and up to date. Every time I receive a new prayer letter I check to see which of the prayer requests have been answered and which requests need to be added. You may even want to send a blank card to a missionary to be filled in and sent back to you. That would be such an encouragement to the missionary, I can tell you!

I don't pray through all of my cards every day – in fact I might pray for one missionary a day or one a week – depending on how many there are. Although

there are some people that I pray for every day, such as
my wife, my family, and myself, the rest of my prayer
cards are included as and when time allows.

There are advantages in keeping a prayer list. Here
are some of them:

- *We have poor memories* – and having a prayer list
  helps us to remember certain people, countries or
  organizations.
- *It assists us with our concentration* – and we can see
  who to pray for and don't waste time thinking, 'Oh,
  what am I going to pray about?'
- *It makes us thankful* – as we see the Lord answer we
  remember to thank him.
- *It helps us to see God at work* – and this in turn
  makes us pray all the more because we see the Lord
  answering our prayers.

*f) wait upon the Lord, he might have something to
say!*

Once I have prayed through my list, and before I end
my prayer time, I sometimes take a moment just to
'wait upon the Lord' to see if he will prompt me to pray
about someone. If someone comes to mind then
(depending on how strongly I feel led) I may give that
person a call to see if they are all right. I tell them that I
had a burden to pray for them, but never pry into their
lives because sometimes God just puts someone on our
heart, not because something is wrong, but just to
encourage that individual.

7

Common Problems

Most people at some point in their Christian life have difficulty in either establishing or maintaining a regular Quiet Time. There can be many reasons for this: some are spiritual, others physical and still others are due to unavoidable circumstances of life. Let us consider some of the common problems which affect our Quiet Times.

missing a Quiet Time!

Although as Christians we know that we are saved by faith and not by works we can still slip into a works mentality when it comes to our Quiet Times. We might miss time with God one day and apologize to him, promising to spend twice as long with him the next day as compensation. The only problem is that when the next day comes we feel obliged to spend twice as long as normal in prayer and if we don't we feel guilty and our time with God becomes a dread rather than a delight.

The solution to feeling guilty in this area is this: don't allow one lapsed day to put you off from approaching God the next. You can't bargain with God and try and win his favour by attempting one hour instead of half an hour. The cross is the only bargaining power we have with God, and he has already accepted that. Just get on and have a Quiet Time the next day! The Lord's faithfulness is new every morning, he remains steadfast even when we don't! (see Lamentations 3:19–23).

feeling unworthy

The Devil does not want you to spend time with God and the two questions that he often sows into our mind regarding time spent in God's presence are these: 'Is it really worth it?' and 'Am I really worth it – will God listen to such an unholy person as me?' The answer is; 'Yes, he will' because even at our holiest moments we are only ever worthy to enter God's presence because of the grace and mercy of the Lord Jesus Christ.

Besides, the very fact that the Devil says 'Is it really worth it?' is proof that it is worth it, because he is the father of all lies (Jn. 8:44). He wants to rob you of that vital contact with God which every Christian needs to remain strong for the battle. So, get on and have your Quiet Time, because God loved you before you ever loved him – or had a Quiet Time in the first place (Rom. 5:8)!

not spending enough quality time on your Quiet Time

This is particularly a problem for those parents with young children who continually feel guilty because they haven't been able to spend quality time with God. They feel as though they have robbed God. The first thing to remember here is that God understands the difficulty of raising children – after all, he has got more than any of us! Not only that, but as parents you are dealing with extra personalities. One of your children might be quiet and easy going, and may play happily in the corner, but another might be very demanding and require constant attention.

God knows that you are juggling your time around, and so you must never feel guilty about taking only

five minutes here or there staggered throughout your working day. Sometimes, the only peace and quiet you get is when you are in the bath! Just take time when you can, the Lord understands. The organized person often struggles the most with feelings of guilt in this area because there is no set time to have a Quiet Time. You may just have to accept the fact that for a few years your 'normal routine' might be not having any routine.

your opinion of God?

There are some Christians who struggle to call God their Heavenly Father because their experience of a father figure at the natural level is full of unhappy memories. Those whose concept of God as their father is of an ogre wanting to beat them with an iron rod will not be too willing to draw near to him. Be assured, if that is your struggle, that God, our Heavenly Father, is the perfection of all that is lacking in those unhappy memories. No father loved like God the Father. Ask him to teach you that love through your Quiet Times.

Sometimes people can feel so ashamed because of sin in their life that they think that it is safer to stand at a distance, or hide behind a bush (like Adam and Eve) rather than draw near to God. They feel that if God is going to say anything to them through his Word it will surely be a message of condemnation that will leave them totally demoralized, rather than refreshed. But remember this, God loves you so much that he would rather have you draw near to him in a mess than you not draw near him at all (Jas. 4:8)!

a dry Quiet Time (it happens to us all!)

Have you ever picked up your Bible and, after reading it for twenty minutes or so, put it down and said, 'What on earth did the Lord say to me through that?' Then you begin to pray and it feels as though your prayers are climbing no higher than the ceiling. If you have experienced something along those lines then you are not alone! What you have experienced is a 'dry Quiet Time'. It can be caused by a number of factors.

a) *mental – the passage we are reading at the time*

Some passages of Scripture are easier to understand and receive something from than others. For instance, we may feel reluctant to read through the Levitical laws day after day because it may feel as if we are wading through legalistic treacle. One tip is to stagger your reading by making sure that every other day you look at an easier passage of Scripture, perhaps something from the Gospels or the Psalms.

b) *physical – tiredness*

Because we are made up of both body and spirit it is understandable that when there is a deficiency in either the physical or the spiritual aspects to our lives this will have a knock-on effect on our devotional lives. As a result, times of physical stress and strain make it harder for us to have the time or energy for our devotions. Always remember that physical tiredness will affect your emotions and your perspective on things – that is why it is best to have a Quiet Time when you are at your brightest.

c) *circumstantial – distractions*

There are always external distractions beyond our control that can affect our devotions: the gas man calls, the children disturb us or the phone rings. These things are unavoidable but they can still put us off our train of thought. We need to remember that when circumstances are against us God is still for us. Try wherever possible to remove yourself from the distractions. If the phone always rings then buy an answering machine, or take the phone off the hook for twenty minutes. Some people wish that they could take their children off the hook for thirty minutes! Regardless of

the distraction, try to return to your devotions as
quickly as possible or, alternatively, postpone your
Quiet Time until later in the day.

d) clinical – liturgical rather than relational

We hear a lot today about repetitive strain injury
where a person can suffer damage to muscles because
they have done exactly the same thing the same way
for hours on end, week in week out. It often creeps
upon a person unawares. There can be a similar type
of condition for the Christian who goes through the
motions of having Quiet Times but receives nothing
from them. Devotions can be reduced to motions
without meaning. When you become aware of this
you need to stop and consider the observation made
by the young man from my youth group: 'Are you just
getting through your Quiet Time or are you engaging
with God?'

If your routine has become just a routine, then try
changing it. That is how workers are prevented from
acquiring repetitive strain injury; they do a different
job for a while. I am not advocating that you give up
on your Quiet Time; instead I suggest that you put
some variety into it so that you don't switch to auto-
matic pilot. The change will probably do you good. It
may be that the use of some pre-set Bible reading notes
will be of some benefit here.

e) spiritual – unconfessed sin in our heart

Unrepented sin or holding a grudge against a fellow
Christian is a sure way of damaging our Quiet Times.

More than anything else it can hinder us from receiving anything from God. Perhaps that is why Jesus said to his disciples: 'And when you stand praying, if you hold anything against anyone, forgive him, so that your Father in heaven may forgive you your sins' (Mk. 11:25). Bitterness can be a barrier to our worship as well as to our prayers. We must learn to keep short accounts with people so that the ungrieved Spirit can work within us. Paul was at pains to emphasize this very point with the church at Ephesus when he wrote:

> And do not grieve the Holy Spirit of God, with whom you were sealed for the day of redemption. Get rid of all bitterness, rage and anger, brawling and slander, along with every form of malice. Be kind and compassionate to one another, forgiving each other, just as in Christ God forgave you (Ephesians 4:30–32).

This is because the Holy Spirit is the most essential person to the believer: he helps us to pray (Rom. 8:26; Jude 20) as well as to live the Christian life (Jn. 14:26; 16:13; Acts 1:8; 2 Cor. 6:6; 2 Tim 1:14). But, because he is a most sensitive person we must be careful not to grieve him. Unconfessed sin and and bitterness will most certainly grieve the Spirit. We therefore need to keep short accounts with our fellow human beings. We must forgive others just as in Christ God forgave us. Failure in this department shows contempt for God's own mercy toward us.

f) confrontational – when God challenges us

When God starts to highlight something in our lives that we are doing wrong, it can sometimes cause us to react in the same way as did Adam and Eve in the garden – we hide! Yet that is the most futile thing we can do precisely because we cannot hide anything from an all-knowing God. 'How', you might say, 'do we hide from God?' We do so quite simply by avoiding his word. If God is challenging an aspect of our lifestyle from the Scriptures then the one thing that we won't want to do is read the Bible, especially if we don't want to change our opinion to agree with his. This is a form of rebellion, and the only way that our hearts can return to the Lord is when we stop wrestling with him and submit to his perfect will for our lives. As long as we live in sin the Lord will never make us feel good about something that he regards as being wrong! But when God does reveal sin in our life we should be thankful that he loves us so much that he won't allow us to get away with anything, otherwise we would grow up to be spoilt, undisciplined children. Always remember that God only highlights things that are wrong in order to change us for the better.

just do it!

'Just do it!' was a slogan I saw printed on someone's T-shirt. I think that it ought to be written into every believer's Bible when it comes to devotional life. There will be times when you won't feel like having a Quiet Time; but remember this golden rule: If you have a Quiet Time and don't get anything out of it, you are still better off than if you had not had a Quiet Time at all! Having a Quiet Time gives God an opportunity to speak to you; not having a Quiet Time almost guarantees his silence! So let us not gag God.

8

Some Tips To Try Out

I want this book to be as practical to the reader as possible so I have included a section which contains helpful suggestions, some of which have been gleaned from the experiences of others. Perhaps you can try out a few.

1. getting up earlier!

I am sure that this is something that we have all vowed to do at one point or another but somehow the dream

never became a reality. Perhaps this was because we tried to achieve too much too soon!

My suggestion is this: don't try to set your alarm one hour or even half an hour early but rather set your alarm to go off just five minutes earlier and keep it like that for two weeks. Then, move it a further five minutes earlier for a further two weeks and so on. You will find that within three months you will be able to get up half an hour earlier, and your body clock has had time to adjust. Obviously in order for this to work effectively you will need to go to bed five minutes earlier in the evening too!

2. invading thoughts

Try writing down all the things that are competing for your mind, such as meetings that you are about to attend, or things that you need to do. This will gradually free your mind from the worry of forgetting those

particular things. Then talk to God about the things written on your 'to do' list, because this too is communion with your Heavenly Father.

3. read the Bible

This may sound rather obvious but I stress this because we can end up reading devotional books, Bible study notes, and commentaries more than we do the Bible itself. Reading devotional books must never take the place of reading the Bible, but ought to be used as a supplementary activity.

4. variety

Make sure that your system does not become a boring routine with no meaning. Remember that you are not talking to a book but to a person. If you are struggling to read God's Word one day, for whatever reason, then talk to him: tell God how frustrated you feel. Always try to verbalize this to God. Oddly enough, this helps you to realize that you are in a relationship, and may well be the means whereby you turn to his word and get something from it.

5. more variety

Try reading a different translation of the Bible alongside your usual version in order to put some freshness into that which is familiar. Other translations that you could look at include: The Message, The Living Bible, NIV or AV.

6. don't race

Don't just try to get through your Bible reading – you get no special medals for speed reading. It is far better for you to look for an encounter with God through one verse than to gain nothing from a whole chapter!

7. keep it moving

Don't spend all your devotional time solely in reading the Bible, or only in prayer. Try to touch on both aspects in some measure. Remember that on some days it will take you more time to settle and prepare your heart and mind than on others. In turn, there may be more things you want to pray for on a particular day than on others.

8. prayer partner

Have a Quiet Time companion or prayer partner (of the same sex) – someone who will ask you once a week or a fortnight how things are going. Find someone who is hungry for God, and who is on your spiritual level. Don't find someone who you want to be counselled by because that leads to spiritual imbalance. The relationship needs to be viewed as a mutual sharing time.

In the Introduction I talked about my Bible college friend, John, who ended up being my Quiet Time companion. John and I found that as we shared what God had been teaching us in our own private devotions we actually prevented each other from getting spiritually dry. If I received little from the Lord one week then John would share what the Lord had taught him and vice versa. The result was that John and I ended up spurring each other on.

Find a Quiet Time companion and you will find that this Scripture will come true: 'As iron sharpens iron, so one man sharpens another' (Prov. 27:17).

9. prayer partners for parents or '9 to 5ers'

Busy mums might benefit from having a Quiet Time companion who is in a similar position to them. Perhaps two or three mums could meet up each week and be Quiet Time companions for each other. They could then tell one another of ways of spending time with the Lord that they have found helpful in their particular situation. Those who have nine-to-five jobs might like to find a Quiet Time companion at their workplace with whom they could meet up either before work or at lunch every so often to encourage one another.

10. take a 'blessing break' during the day

Why not pray for someone while you are having your coffee break? Take your prayer cards to work with you and pray during those redundant moments of time that we all have during the day: at the bus stop, on the train, in a lift, or even while waiting for someone to answer the phone! Use these as extra opportunities to pray. Nehemiah was one who often sent up arrow prayers whilst he worked (Neh. 2:4).

11. have a 'Quiet Day'

If you have never tried this then I would highly recommend it. Every three or four months set aside a day (or half a day) as a Quiet Day with God. Head out to the hills by yourself with a picnic. Take your Bible, a note pad and begin to talk to the Lord and analyse where you are going with your life. Use this time to review and amend your priorities as well as your prayer cards so that you have fresh cards for the next few months. More often than not on these Quiet Days I spend much of the time in fresh surrender to the Lord.

12. blessings from the past!

You might find it helpful to make a list of verses of Scripture that are pertinent to you. Many people highlight or underline passages in their Bibles from which they have received blessings in the past. I do and it is to those very same verses that I tend to turn when suffering from spiritual depletion. More often than not a blessing from the past becomes a lifeline for the present. You need to build up some reserves of Scripture for the dry patches, in advance.

13. getting to work early!

If you would like to have your Quiet Time in the morning but are conscious of being late for work because of traffic, then try leaving early so that you arrive at work half hour before everyone else does.

That way you can have a Quiet Time in the office
before everyone else arrives. This may also be a means
of witnessing to your work-mates if they ever ask you
why you are in early!

14. meet in a museum – or anywhere else that is quiet!

If you work in the city centre then why not find a quiet
place like the local museum, a park, a library, or a
church to spend some time with the Lord in relative
quiet?

15. food for thought

Why not use your lunch break to chew over the Word
of God as well as your sandwich! Indeed, you could
eat your breakfast and have your Bible open on the
table at the same time. That would give a whole new
meaning to the verse, 'Man does not live on bread
alone' (Mt. 4:4).

16. read and digest a letter

Why not set aside some time on a Sunday afternoon
just to read an entire letter from the New Testament –
after all, that was the way it was intended to be read!

My wife and I once did this when we turned up to a
church too early (well, miracles do happen!). We
decided to read, out loud, through Paul's letter to the

Ephesians from start to finish, taking a chapter each. It took us about twenty minutes reading at a slow but steady pace. We then asked ourselves:

- Why was this written?
- What are the main things that Paul was trying to communicate?
- Are there any verses that stand out as particularly encouraging or challenging to us?

It was so refreshing to read right through a whole letter – we really got the flow of what the author was intending. This is a particularly useful exercise if you are about to embark on a devotional study of a particular book or letter. Why not try this? One Sunday afternoon read through the letter to the Ephesians at one sitting. Then for the following two weeks, take the natural divisions in the letter (there are about twelve of them) and slowly read and meditate on a section a day. As you read make a special note of a verse, phrase, theme or word that you think God might like you to take with you throughout the day. Perhaps write down one verse to memorize for the week.

17. God's word to you

Try inserting your name into certain passages of Scripture? Here is an example of one that I tried recently:

> Love is patient, love is kind. It does not envy, it does not boast, it is not proud. It is not rude, it is not self-seeking, it is not easily angered, it keeps no record of wrongs.

Love does not delight in evil but rejoices with the truth. It always protects, always trusts, always hopes, always perseveres (1 Corinthians 13:4–7).

I figured that these were qualities that the Lord would want for every believer, so I substituted my name in place of the word 'love'. It made humbling and challenging reading! Try inserting your name as you read it. Here are a few others to try: Jeremiah 31:3; Ephesians 1:3–23; James 1: 2–4.

18. your turn

I know of one couple who each take turns to look after the children while the other goes off to have a Quiet Time. This is particularly important for the mother who may have had no time on her own throughout the whole day. No doubt I shall have more ideas on this once I have children! I also know of one parent who gets her children involved in her Quiet Times. She encourages them to pray briefly and reads her passage of Scripture with them. Obviously their attention span is limited, but at least it is something. Besides, they are learning a good habit at an early age!

19. one for the road

If you spend a lot of time in the car, why not buy a copy of Spurgeon's *Morning & Evening* (or any short devotional) and tape your own voice reading them into a tape recorder? In half an hour you should be able to tape about a dozen or so 'thoughts for the day'. Then you can use them in conjunction with some worship tapes to help you to focus on the Lord as you travel, just like on the road to Emmaus! One tip: Learn to pray with your eyes open! Alternatively, you could record yourself reading one of Paul's letters which takes about twenty minutes to do. This could also be done on a personal stereo so that you can listen whilst you are walking to work or out hiking in the hills.

20. using your imagination

God has given us a wonderful imagination and sometimes it is worth using it to picture the sights, sounds and atmosphere of some of the Bible incidents. For instance, what would you see and feel if you were in the boat when the storm was raging around you? Would you have reacted differently from the disciples? How do you feel before, during and after Jesus calms the storm? Now relate that story to a storm that is currently happening in your life. How do you think that Jesus will deal with the storm or with you? Can you trust him with your present situation? The chances are that if you are an artistic person this exercise may appeal to you and if you are not, then it won't.

21. question time

It is sometimes helpful to have some key questions at the back of your mind when considering a passage of Scripture. They will help you to dig out some nuggets of gold from God's word for yourself. For instance, as you read a passage of Scripture consider these questions.

- What is happening in this passage?
- Why is it happening?
- What can I learn from this passage?
- Is there a truth I need to apply?
- Is there a promise that I can keep?
- Is there an action I need to take?
- Is there a habit I need to stop?
- Is there an encouragement I can take?
- Is there a sin I need to confess?

- Is there something about God that I need to learn?
- Is there a challenge to my life and lifestyle?

You may want to keep a journal of the things that God teaches you from his Word.

22. Bible study notes

Bible study notes can often give you helpful background information about a passage. They can also help you to develop a structure to your Quiet Time by directing what you read, giving you a short devotional thought and guiding your prayers. They usually take between ten and twenty minutes to go through. Try to choose study notes that go through a book or theme at a time rather than doing scriptural gymnastics as you leap all over the place.

23. read a hymn

Why not begin your devotional time by reading the
words of a hymn or a chorus to help you consider
the majesty of the God whose presence you are entering? I find hymns especially helpful as they are full of
wonderful and inspiring truths about God that
encourage us to draw near to God with confidence.
Besides, many hymns are like mini sermons, carrying
both doctrine and theology in song.

24. listen to a worship tape

Being a musician I occasionally start my devotions by
singing some worship songs to the Lord as a means of
preparing my heart prior to reading and praying. For
those of you who are not musicians then why not listen to a song or two from a worship tape, preferably
looking at the words as you listen. Scripture does after
all tell us to 'Speak to one another with psalms, hymns
and spiritual songs' (Eph. 5:19a).

25. what to pray about?

I have met people who say, 'Once I have prayed for
myself and my family I can't think of anything else to
pray about!' If that describes you, then take heart;
there is loads to pray about. For a start, why not listen
to the news headlines and make a note of prayer items
on a national and international scale? Subscribe to

some missionary organizations who will supply you with ample prayer material. Try praying for people in your congregation, using the church members' list to prompt you. Why not listen out to the needs of your work colleagues, approach them privately and ask if they would mind if you prayed about their situation? This provides a tremendous evangelistic opportunity!

That should be enough to get you started. If you get stuck for something to pray about for a missionary then simply pray something for them that you are currently praying for yourself (after all they are human like you, not superhuman). Or perhaps use a verse that encouraged you from your Quiet Time as a blessing or promise that you want them to know in their own life.

26. too much to pray about!

As you get on in the Christian faith you soon discover that there is so much to pray about and so little time to do the praying. I don't know about you but I seem to receive two or three prayer letters from various organizations each week! The problem is that every one of them has valid prayer requests and one feels guilty just throwing the prayer letter in the bin. What do you do? A friend of mine told me that he reads the letter there and then and spends about five to ten minutes earnestly praying for the requests mentioned. Then he screws up the prayer letter, throws it in the bin, and forgets about it! That example is worth serious consideration, for I believe that a missionary would rather have you pray earnestly for them for ten minutes than not pray at all and collect a catalogue of prayer letters as well as whole lot of guilt! One has to be realistic and ruthless at the same time in this area.

9

A Prayer Guide Based On
The Lord's Prayer

It has been said that the prayer which we know as 'the
Lord's Prayer' really ought to be entitled 'the disciples' prayer' because the Lord intended it to be used
by his disciples. The prayer was designed to be a
model for our own praying, a skeleton prayer which
we can flesh out. Within it we see every element
which all prayer ought to contain: praise, thanksgiving, confession and supplication. In this chapter I
have divided up the words of that 'disciples' prayer'
and expanded upon each phrase to show my thought
processes as I slowly pray through this prayer using it
as a model. The words in italics simply show you
what I might pray as I am prompted by each phrase,
though I am sure that you can express things better in
your own words.

'Our Father who art in heaven'

Thank God for who he is. *Thank you, Lord that we
can indeed call you Father. In you we find our true*

*identity, sense of value and belonging. You are our
provider and our protector. You dwell in heaven and
yet care for us here on earth.*

'Hallowed be thy name'

Pray that in your life today you will bring honour to
God. *You are the great eternal God who is worthy of
all honour and praise. Therefore, may my life today
bring you joy, and may everything I do and say be
honouring to you and bring glory to your name.*

'Thy kingdom come'

Pray for the rule of God in individual human lives as
well as in homes, communities and nations. *Lord, I
pray that your glorious kingdom will continue to
extend throughout the world as you bring more people into a saving knowledge of your son Jesus. May I
always look forward to, and be ready for, the day
when your kingdom will come with its full power and
majesty.*

'Thy will be done, on earth as it is in heaven'

Pray for decisions that you are about to take concerning work, family, finance, relationships and the
future. Ask God that these might be according to his
will rather than simply your own desire. Pray for your

work place that Godly principles would be carried out there and that management decisions would be honest and fair. Pray also that the Government might make decisions that honour the Lord. Then turn your attention to parts of the world suffering injustice or war. Pray for one or two specific situations that have come up in the news.

'Give us this day our daily bread'

Thank the Lord for his provision in the many things that we can so easily take for granted. *Lord, I thank you for the spiritual and material comforts that you have entrusted me with. I thank you for the daily provision of everything that I need to live. Every good gift is from you and I thank you for that.*

'And forgive us our sins'

At this point take time to examine your behaviour, actions and attitudes to see if there is anything that the Lord does not approve of. Then ask his forgiveness for not having behaved in a God-honouring way. Ask him to forgive you for any unkind thought or word that you have said to, or about, others. And pray for the opportunity to make amends and restore any broken relationship.

Lord forgive me for . . .

'As we forgive those who have sinned against us'

Take time to reflect on any who have consciously or
unconsciously offended you, and ask the Lord to give
you the grace to forgive them. Ask the Lord to help
you to treat those people as though they had never
offended you at all! (That might be hard to do, but if
you do it you will be acting in a Christ-like manner.
Remember, holding a grudge cripples us as well as
others.)

*Lord, I forgive . . . for . . . Help me not to hold a
grudge against them so that my walk with you is not
spoiled.*

'And lead us not into temptation'

Ask the Lord to give you the strength to avoid sin and
to assist you to throw out unhelpful invading thoughts
which might cause you to stray from his ways (2 Cor.
10:4–5).
    Pray that the Holy Spirit would highlight anything
you watch, read or do which might cause you to stum-
ble. Ask the Lord to show you if there are any
unhealthy relationships which he would not approve
of.

*Lord, guard my heart from straying from you will-
ingly or unwillingly, and give me strength to avoid
acting upon any unhelpful thoughts.*

'But deliver us from evil'

Ask the Lord to protect you from the work of the evil one, and for deliverance from any attack of the Devil. Remember that 'the one who is in you is greater than the one who is in the world' (1 Jn. 4:4). The Devil has power, but it is a limited power, whereas the Lord God Almighty has unlimited power, and through the blood of Jesus the power of the Devil has been overcome. The Devil has been disarmed so that even death has lost its power over us (1 Cor. 15:55; Col. 2:15; Rev. 12:11).

'For thine is the kingdom, the power and the glory, for ever and ever, Amen'

The Lord's kingdom, power and glory are unsurpassed. They are eternal and almighty and shall not be overcome. This is the God who we are privileged to call our Father, and who walks with us through every step of our lives and into every situation we will ever face.

10

Praying Through The Psalms

During times of trouble or heartache, Christians have turned to the Psalms more than to any other book in the Bible. This is because in the Psalms we find such raw honesty. We find people being 'honest to God' and telling him their deepest thoughts, just as they are, without any window-dressing. In the Psalms we find a kindred spirit, a true mirror of our own soul's questions, doubts, struggles and desires. The psalmists say the kind of things that we ourselves long to say but never feel that we can. We find it hard to approach the Almighty with our fears and doubts in the way that they did – but the truth of the matter is that we can!

Howard Baker says that in the Psalms:

God Himself had supplied a toolbox for constructing a meaningful prayer life. All of the formulas, acrostics and gimmicks to make praying simple and easy are exposed as shallow in the face of the pulsating reality, life and depth of the Psalms as a guide to prayer. I learn to pray by praying, and the Psalms provide the pattern for me. As I pray the Psalms leave their mark on my soul until finally

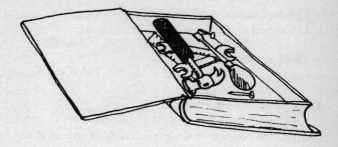

I find my own prayers conforming to the original pattern (Baker, 1997).

There are four things about prayer that the Psalms teach us:

i) pray honestly

We are taught to pray honestly about our true feelings and emotional state. There is no need for us to disguise our emotional state before the Lord. We can come to him with all the conflicts, fears and doubts in the world, as Charlotte Elliott discovered when she wrote the hymn 'Just as I am'.

Just as I am, without one plea,
But that thy blood was shed for me,
And that thou bidst me come to thee,
O Lamb of God, I come. (verse 1)

Just as I am, though tossed about
With many a conflict, many a doubt,

Fightings within and fears without,
O Lamb of God, I come. (verse 3)

Charlotte Elliott, 1789–1871

ii) pray comprehensively

The Psalms contain a wide spectrum of material to focus our prayers upon. For instance, we are encouraged to pray about the state of the nations (Ps. 2); to confess and repent of our sinfulness (Ps. 51); to seek forgiveness and cleansing (Ps. 32); to exalt God's glory and splendour (Ps. 8; 19); to praise God (Ps. 24; 33; 47); to find security in him (Ps. 3; 20; 23; 34); to pray against injustice (Ps. 12; 43) and the ungodly (Ps. 14); to give thanks (Ps. 21); to express our longings (Ps. 42). And that is just in the first fifty psalms!

iii) pray in a God-centred way

Often our prayers can be rather introspective, focusing only upon ourselves, our problems, our needs and our desires. Yet we need to remember that God is infinitely bigger than our problems and therefore ought to be the main focal point.

Many psalmists begin with their whole vision consumed with the issues that they are facing. These fill their whole horizon to the extent that they cannot see beyond the problem. But once God is included in the picture he begins to eclipse the problems. He floods the darkness of the soul with penetrating brightness.

He alone brings hope, so that by the end of the psalm the problems are viewed in their true perspective and are no longer larger than the God who aids the believer. As a result the psalmist bows in adoration with an uplifted heart knowing that, although the problems are large and may not disappear easily, the God whom he worships is larger still and will never leave him.

iv) pray responsively

Not only do the psalms provide us with the basis of our approach to God, they also teach us a right response. We are to say thank you to God, we are to repent of sin, we are to walk in his ways, we are to praise him, we are to serve him wholeheartedly. In this way our prayer invokes a response not just from God, but from us too.

Why not examine the structure of the Psalms to see if you can identify some of these points?

(Concept taken from an article by Howard Baker in the magazine *Christianity*, October 1997.)

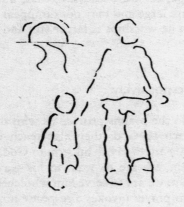

11

My Own Walk With God

By nature I am an extrovert and for me, as for many extroverts, the idea of solitude away from contact with other human beings can, at times, be rather difficult. Extroverts generally have their batteries recharged by being with people and introverts by solitude away from people. In addition to being an extrovert I am also a person who is task driven, which can be a distraction to my own devotions in that my natural tendency is to want to get on and do things for the Lord rather than spending time praying about the tasks with the Lord himself. That is something which I constantly have to guard against and I have been greatly helped by the psalmist, who reminds me that 'Unless the Lord builds the house, its builders labour in vain' (Ps. 127:1).

Generally speaking my tendency is to have my devotions first thing in the morning after breakfast. I do this for two reasons. First, I know that if I don't have them first thing in the morning I will find it diffi-cult (though not impossible) to reschedule them to another slot in the day simply because for me, as for most people, free time becomes harder to find as the day progresses. The second reason is that my mind is at its sharpest in the mornings immediately after I have eaten something. Besides, there are enough unpredictable distractions in life without my introducing the extra distraction of a rumbling stomach!

What I actually do varies. Usually I begin my devotional times by sitting in my favourite chair downstairs. I prepare my heart to meet with God by doing one of three things: I either read a hymn or a short devotion from Charles Spurgeon's *Cheque Book of the Bank of Faith* or sing a few worship songs on the guitar. I do this because many hymns are basically theology in song, and the words stem from the composers' own encounter with God. They were inspired by either a scriptural truth, an attribute of God's character, or a response to his mercy and love. They were, if you like, written to encourage people to remember that God is worth singing about and praising. My heart is therefore immediately excited by someone else's inspiration which rubs something off on me so that I end up nodding my head in agreement with the writer's words, as if to say 'Yes, that is the God whose presence I am privileged to enter!' Depending on how sluggish my mind is I may take five minutes just preparing myself in this way prior to reading God's word.

I tend then to move on to my Bible reading. Generally I alternate between Old and New Testaments, reading a chapter from a book from start to finish. I prefer this systematic approach as it assists me to get to grips with each book of the Bible rather than playing scriptural gymnastics leaping here, there and everywhere. As I read I consciously ask the Lord to illuminate my mind by his Holy Spirit as I read his word.

I have been using the same Bible for my devotions for over ten years now and I will always have a pen and highlighter in my hand ready to underline a verse or word which stands out for me. If a reading has a particularly poignant significance to my life and situation then I occasionally jot down the encouragement I received from reading that particular verse. One could say that my Bible is a living journal of God's speaking into my life. It is my hope that one day (God willing) my children might gain some insight into their father's relationship with the Lord through the notes that I have made there.

As I read, my eye is constantly on the look-out for a truth about God, an attitude I need to adopt, or a lesson I need to learn from the reading and I hardly ever read a passage where one or more of these fails to draw something from the well of Scripture. The reading itself often prompts me to pray for myself or others as I proceed. If it is a particularly rich passage of Scripture I may only dwell on a few verses rather than attempting simply to get through my chapter. After all, the whole aim is for God to speak to me and if he says something in the first verse that challenges me then it would be impertinent of me to say, 'Hang on, God, I haven't finished my chapter yet!' I need to seize the blessing, the wisdom or the rebuke as soon as the Holy Spirit illuminates it, and then to seed that word deep into my heart before it is snatched away.

Occasionally I change from my routine and use a set of Bible study notes to guide and prompt my reading. I find this quite refreshing as a good set of notes asks questions and presents challenges that I might not have thought about myself. It is almost like having someone sitting there with you during your devotions sharing insights on the passage.

Having read a portion of Scripture I then turn to prayer. For this, as I have said earlier, I use prayer cards that I keep in a little folder slotted into my Bible. They contain names and prayer requests of family, friends, work colleagues, missionaries, and people who need to know Christ, and are there to prompt me in prayer. The notes and requests that I have written down on the cards are not the prayers themselves, otherwise my prayer would become rather liturgical and flat. I try as far as possible to pray for people as though I have never prayed for them before – even though they are constantly on my prayer list. I try to obtain a photograph of them so that they are right in front of me as I pray.

If there is insufficient time to pray for people I slip my prayer cards into my pocket and take them with me as I travel to work. There will always be redundant moments either on a bus, in a waiting room or in a lay-by that enable me to pull them out and pray for a few more people.

Usually I pray for myself last of all, mainly because my Bible reading itself has already prompted me to pray for myself in terms of confession, thanksgiving and supplication. My tendency is to pray about meetings with people and other engagements on the way to the appointment itself, especially if I am walking to it. This helps me to ask the Lord for his wisdom and insight for the immediate situation I am about to enter, besides emphasizing all the more that it is not a question of 'Here I go', but rather one of 'We are in this together, Lord. Here *we* go!'

An important factor for me in my devotional life is to have a regular time with the Lord but to have a great deal of variety within that regular time. As a result I employ a number of the different suggestions made in this book, the combinations of which would be too numerous to put into writing. This maintains discipline and consistency whilst retaining freshness. The one factor I always persevere with is to meet with God through my devotions and have him speak to me.

12

Other People's Devotions

Elsie Harris – missionary, wife and mother

When I came to faith in the Lord Jesus at about the age of ten, I was carefully discipled, for which I am truly thankful. I remember my first ever Scripture Union daily reading card, purchased for a penny back in 1937, with readings for a whole year. This was a junior card, so the readings were very short but it started me on the road in the habit of a daily Quiet Time. I also attended an S.U. Monday evening class where I was helped to find my way around the whole Bible, and encouraged to learn by heart two verses of Scripture a week.

As I grew to know the Lord Jesus, so my appetite for his word increased. A Quiet Time became as important to me spiritually, as daily food to the physical body. During the war years, from the age of twelve, I learned to pray more fervently, and know that the Lord's presence was with me when I was an evacuee from London, and in the midst of physical danger. My Quiet Times matured as a result of that experience.

My first job was in an office in a nine-to-five job, and it was relatively easy to maintain a Quiet Time. I chose the early morning as the best time for me. Later, when nursing, with irregular hours and night duty, I had to adjust my times. I must have slipped up sometimes, due to long hours and tiredness, but my desire was always to meet with Jesus in the 'secret place', which for me was my bedroom. At Bible college in later years, I had the privilege of deeper study of the word and used devotional books, commentaries and a concordance to assist me in drawing more from my Bible reading.

When I became a missionary overseas, and a wife, and eventually a mother, I again had to be flexible concerning the time I had my devotions, but no day was right without this time apart with my saviour and Lord. My husband read the same passage as me, separately, then we met later to share what the Lord had said to us both. So our married life was enriched. When he was away on safari, we continued reading the same passages, and this kept us close to each other, in the Lord. At breakfast times, we read from *Daily Light*, when possible, and put the birth dates of family and friends near the dates, so that we could remember them specially in prayer on their special day.

Now I am a widow and a senior citizen, so I have more time to choose my daily timetable, and my Quiet Times are even more precious. I usually have about forty-five minutes before breakfast, when I read a psalm (usually as an act of worship) and a chapter from the Old Testament followed by one from the New. When I pray I follow various mission prayer calendars for the day as well as praying for my family and friends. I have a pattern, so that each one is prayed for at least once a week, and some, every day. I also have a daily 'emergency' prayer list for pressing things brought to my attention. In addition the BBC news often provides me with world issues that I turn into prayer.

After breakfast, I usually have several prayer letters arrive in the post, and these I read sitting in my favourite armchair in the living room. I then take the contents of each letter to the Lord in prayer, and sometimes go over previous missionary prayer letters and remember again the needs that they have. I also try to write to someone overseas each day to encourage them in their ministry.

I have used various systems for Bible reading and prayer over the years; more recently I have followed the *One Year Bible*, which includes a chapter from Proverbs as well as a psalm and OT and NT readings.

I have recently acquired the *One Year Hymn Book*, which gives a hymn for each day and outlines how it came to be written. I greatly enjoy using this. Sunday afternoons provide more opportunities to pray for missionaries and others, and sometimes a friend will join me for that time so that we can pray together. Then there are the times of talking to the Lord, when I am out walking, or on the bus, praying for those that are on my heart. Some call these 'telephone prayers'.

This may all sound easy to do, but in practice it is not so: prayer is hard work, and we are in a spiritual battle against a strong, relentless enemy who constantly attacks with doubts, apathy and busyness. But Jesus is the victor, and he has told us to pray. A Quiet Time is vital to me.

Elsie Harris

This account shows the importance of discipleship and discipline. Elsie is a woman of prayer, and many people know that they can rely upon her to bear their burden before the Lord. Yet if it hadn't been for that person who faithfully discipled Elsie in making her Quiet Time a priority she may never have been the pillar of prayer that she is today. Elsie's life reveals how her habit of a regular Quiet Time has been virtually impossible to break despite the varying seasons of life. She has resolved in her will to meet with her Lord and when you make a resolve like that you will find the necessary time to keep your appointment.

Andy Kneale – a regional sales manager

The best place to start is with who I am and the lifestyle and job that I have. I am 37, married to Ruth and have two children, Rachel, aged ten, and Matthew, aged nine. I am employed as a regional sales manager for a printing company on the South Coast of England.

Over the years I have discovered, and have been told, that I am the type of person who enjoys a little space each day, and so, although my lifestyle might seem a little sedate to some, to me it is jam packed. If you include the things that I do in church, such as playing in a worship group and attending a house-group, as well as being a father, then life at times can get a little strained.

In my job there is no such thing as a typical day, as each day brings its own challenges in various ways. I am never surprised if I need to wake at 5 a.m. in order to get to my office for a 10 a.m. meeting. My day continues with three or four appointments and the mobile phone ringing almost constantly. I usually return home between 6.30 p.m. and 8 p.m. After briefly tucking the children into bed and reading them stories I then try to finish writing up the day's work, which can potentially go on until 9 p.m. or 10 p.m.

I have enough time to say 'Hello' to Ruth and spend a little time with her before wearily dragging myself upstairs to bed. Anyone who is thinking of becoming a 'rep' should think hard and long as it is not all it is cracked up to be!

I am not a morning person so I find it difficult to have my Quiet Time early on. Similarly, as my days are so hectic and long I usually find that I am not an evening person either. So how do I get round the problem with regards to my devotional time?

I have found that since most of my working life is spent in a car, travelling about 1,000 miles each week, the best use of my time is to have my devotions during that part of the day when I am on the road. I have needed to learn a few tricks to keep me on the road spiritually and to stop me from veering off into some poor unsuspecting pedestrian. So, for half an hour, I turn off my mobile telephone, switch off the radio and turn on the tape player. My usual routine then begins with my listening to the Bible on tape, meditating upon a couple of verses or a passage and applying that truth or promise to my situation. Then I pray (with my eyes open!), usually out loud, as that helps me to concentrate. Then I use a prayer card that I keep in the glove compartment, on which I have listed friends, family, or people that I know of who are experiencing difficulty, or who need to come to Christ for salvation. I use this as a prompt to help me focus my prayers and so that I do not forget to pray for an individual.

Other things that I use from time to time are worship tapes to sing along to and meditate upon the words. I also use a Navigators' Topical Memory Verse System to help me memorize passages of Scripture. Monday is usually a good day for meditating upon the Sunday sermon as it is still fresh in my mind.

In addition to the things mentioned above I also like to read a devotional book. The book that I am using at present is Al Denson's *Take Me to the Cross* (Tyndale House). This is a 45-day study book which looks at different topics that can affect our relationship with God. It also has a fantastic section, '45 Awesome Principles to Live by'. The studies themselves are approximately three to four pages long, consisting of an introduction to the topic, followed by a short question and study time which finishes with pointers for prayer and ideas for further study. I find this a very practical book that is easy to read and use.

Although I can worship, pray and meditate whilst driving, I have not mastered the art of driving whilst doing a Bible study. So for that I usually find a lay-by or side road where I can park safely, although this too has its risks . . . as I discovered one day.

I was parked in a small road in Cheshire. It was just an ordinary village with houses on each side of the road. 'Perfect!' I thought, and proceeded to have my Quiet Time. Unaware of the passing of time, I found to my horror that a police car had pulled alongside mine and a rather officious officer proceeded to ask me all sorts of questions about why I had been sitting in my car for an hour and a half. One of the local residents had thought that I was up to no good and had decided to call the police – after all, I was sitting outside a bank! I explained that I was reading my Bible, and showed the officer what I was studying. He then told me that he too was a Christian and that he was sorry for interrupting my study, and he went on his way.

I realize that my Quiet Times are not to everyone's taste, but they fit in perfectly with my lifestyle. If I hear people say that they are too busy to pray or have a Quiet Time, I always feel the need to speak out, as I believe that if you truly desire to meet with God each day, then you can always make time – however short.

After all, what state would we be in if God never had time for us!

Andy Kneale

Andy's approach shows the versatility that one needs to have in some occupations in order to meet with the Lord. You know, in the Bible times the Lord told the people to remember his commands in many different ways, one of which was to talk about them as they travelled along the road (Deut. 6:6–9; 11:18–20; Lk. 24:13–32). If you are desperate enough to meet with the Lord you will find the ways and the means to do so.

Sarah – a busy mum

The following testimony is from a young mother who, for the purposes of this book, we will call Sarah. Just to set the scene, Sarah is a married mother at home with two pre-school children, Paul, aged five, and Miriam, aged three. Miriam is a bright, fun-loving girl who suffers from cerebral palsy; as a result she needs more care, attention and therapy in order to achieve her best in life. Sarah's husband John works for a packaging company.

I have been a Christian for over ten years. Before having children I used to have regular daily devotions in the morning. This provided me with encouragement, guidance and an opportunity to pray for others. When my first child, Paul, was born I managed to have consistent, though less frequent, Quiet Times while Paul was asleep. I had to learn to abandon the housework in order to stop for a short time to spend time alone with God. I would read a chapter or a paragraph from the Scriptures, then pray using a note book in which I would record my thoughts and prayer requests and the Lord's answers.

However, after the birth of our daughter Miriam, John and I entered into a bleak and emotional time for over two years. The work-load and stress placed upon us by Miriam's condition were enormous as we struggled emotionally with all the 'Why?' and 'How?' questions surrounding Miriam. As a result, my husband's and my own Quiet Times were plunged into their darkest moments. They were more often than not full of tears and frustration.

Our spiritual input during much of the time was through the love of others from our church and God's grace shown to us through their kindness. We were reassured by God's promise 'Never will I leave you; never will I forsake you' (Hebrews 13:5). People would sometimes come round and pray with us, often in direct response to our pain. Throughout this time we felt very loved and cared for both by our church and by our families.

Our faith developed and deepened astonishingly through this experience. God's grace often arrives in our hearts at just the time we need it most. We read the Bible, often seeking encouragement and comfort from it. I found that reading the Psalms in particular was a challenge and a comfort to me. We prayed many 'help' prayers for ourselves, and we did try to pray for others even though it was very haphazard.

Most of my energy goes into loving and caring for my family; Miriam takes a lot of it. What is left over is for my own spiritual devotions and pastimes and for serving others. In a sense I have given up my liberty because of Miriam. I regard what is left of my time as the Lord's to do with as he wishes! Sometimes I yearn for the independence that I see other families have, but I know that my calling is different from theirs. I view every act of care and patience with Miriam, and also with Paul and John, as my act of worship to God through my actions. I know that that is acceptable and pleasing to God. If I can't find much time or energy for Quiet Times then I ask the Lord to accept my work as an act of love and reverence to him.

Of course I do need close times with God to reflect and pray. But between 7 a.m. and 8 p.m. there is not much peace and quiet! Besides, Miriam needs constant supervision and my attention is turned to her nearly all the time. Having a family member with a disability is very tiring and stressful. It can be relentlessly draining both physically and emotionally, and it can also be incredibly isolating too. I often feel alone in my daily tasks, but I know that the Lord is there to share the loneliness.

Sometimes I have a Quiet Time before I go to sleep. I read a passage in the Bible and pray for a short time. I tend to vary my reading between Old and New Testaments so that I touch upon every part of the Bible. When I pray I usually try to come before the Lord with a confession, or honestly to tell him of my struggles. Then I pray for others. I usually pray for people who I know from my church fellowship in addition to my own family. I often pray for a missionary and try to pray specifically for a few people, using their most recent newsletter. My Quiet Times usually last ten minutes and I might only have a few in a week or a fortnight. Despite this rather inconsistent pattern I find that these times are moving and refreshing. God speaks to me more often than when I had many consistent Quiet Times. I think that this is due to my personal experience since Miriam's birth and the many times I have cried out to God. The Lord knows the work I do and how unrelenting it is, and he blesses me with grace when I need it most.

Due to the lack of regular 'spiritual meals' I have had to adapt to get fed in a different way. For instance, I pray to the Lord as I push the pushchair or wash up. I try to be prayerful in my thoughts and practice so that I don't just think of someone, I pray for them, too. Throughout my day, rather like Nehemiah, I send up many ICPM (Inter Continental Prayer Missiles). I place some verse cards on the kitchen window-sill to look at and leave missionary prayer letters around the house to prompt me to pray for them.

I have thought a lot about Daniel and the three other Hebrew princes taken captive in Babylon and how they remained strong on a diet of vegetables and water. My husband and I are on this sort of spiritual diet – long term – and it amazes me how God imparts so much grace to us and how he keeps us spiritually healthy despite out difficult circumstances.

I know that I need bigger 'spiritual meals', when I can spend more leisurely time singing, worshipping, meditating and examining God's word, but for the time being that is not possible. I ask the Lord constantly that I will remain as hungry for him when I have more time and space in future years.

Sarah

There is no doubt that Sarah and John's life experience is quite different from that of most of us. Indeed, I don't think that any of us can fully appreciate the liberty, flexibility and time that we currently have until it is removed from us. Having a child like Miriam inevitably takes away much of that freedom. Yet, despite this, both Sarah and John have learned to adapt their lives physically, spiritually and emotionally to accommodate those circumstances. They have learned to turn mundane tasks into worship and fleeting moments of quiet into prayer and praise. The heart-cry of Sarah is that she will remain as hungry for God when she has more time on her hands. I pray that the Lord will one day grant her and John the space that they once had years ago. But I also pray that her story might inspire all of us to make good use of the time that we have now while it is still available to us.

Quiet Time Studies

Study 1 Priorities and Distractions

PREPARE YOUR HEART

Before you begin write down on a piece of paper anything that is distracting you at this moment: perhaps a meeting you need to attend, someone you need to see, or something you have to do. Write down anything that might rob you of these next few moments with God. Now lay that card down and carry on with the rest of this short study.

Take a moment to reflect upon the words of this song.

Be still, my soul: the Lord is on thy side;
Bear patiently the cross of grief or pain;
Leave to thy God to order and provide;
In every change He faithful will remain.
Be still, my soul, thy best, thy heavenly Friend
Through thorny ways leads to a joyful end.

Be still, my soul: thy God doth undertake
To guide the future as He has the past.
Thy hope, thy confidence, let nothing shake;
All now mysterious shall be bright at last.
Be still, my soul: the waves and winds still know
His voice who ruled them while He dwelt below.

Be still, my soul, the hour is hastening on
When we shall be forever with the Lord,
When disappointment, grief and fear are gone,
Sorrow forgot, love's purest joys restored.
Be still, my soul: when change and tears are past,
All safe and blessed we shall meet at last.

Katharina von Schlegel, b. 1697
tr. by Jane Laurie Borthwick, 1813–97

READ GOD'S WORD

Lk. 10:38–42

If this passage had ended at verse 40 what would your
initial reaction have been? Would you have viewed
Mary as lazy and Martha as godly? When we see the
Lord's reaction to Martha's plea 'Tell her to help me!'
we see a different perspective: that it is possible to do
many things for the Lord and not spend adequate time
with the Lord.

> *'All work for the Lord ought to be devotional.'*

Yes, the 'many things' do need to get done, but not to
the detriment of spending time with the Lord. The

Lord wasn't condemning Martha for working but for overworking, doing more than she ought to have done, which squeezed out precious moments with him.

Reflect: It is possible to overfill our diaries so that we become too tired, too busy and too late for the Lord. How is your diary looking? Is there anything you need to pull out of? Are all your appointments God's appointments?

> *'We can always find time for the things that we most want to do!'*

The many things that vie for our attention can distract us from quality time with the Lord. Try re-examining your priorities for today and see if you need to make some adjustments. We can all find plenty of things to keep us busy, but the question is are they the most important?

PRAY

Confess to the Lord if you have been overworking or robbing him of time.

Ask the Lord to help you to prioritize your life better.

Bring to the Lord the things that you have written on your card.

Pray for other people in your church who may be overworked.

Study 2 Burn-out!

PREPARE YOUR HEART

Depending on how much time you have, begin your devotion either by listening to one or two worship songs or by reading the words of the hymn below. Then reflect for a moment on the question.

'We rest on Thee,' our Shield and our Defender!
We go not forth alone against the foe;
Strong in Thy strength, safe in Thy keeping tender,
'We rest on Thee, and in Thy Name we go.'

Yes 'in Thy name,' O captain of salvation!
In Thy dear Name, all other names above:
Jesus our Righteousness, our sure Foundation,
Our Prince of glory and our King of love.

We go in faith, our own great weakness feeling,
And needing more each day Thy grace to know:
Yet from our hearts a song of triumph pealing;
'We rest on Thee, and in Thy name we go.'

'We rest on Thee,' our Shield and our Defender!
Thine is the battle, Thine shall be the praise;
When passing through the gates of pearly splendour,
Victors – we rest with Thee, through endless days.

Edith Gilling Cherry, 1872–1897

'Where is your sense of value in God's sight found? Is it in what you do or in who you are?'

READ GOD'S WORD

1 Kings 19:1–18

Elijah, that great prophet of God, had just won a tremendous victory against the priests who worshipped the false god Baal. As a result, over 450 prophets of Baal had been executed by the people who had then returned once more to the worship of the God of the Bible. In addition to this Elijah had had the faith to pray for rain even though none had fallen for over three years (see 1 Kings 18:16–46). Yet despite all that we find Elijah in a desperately low state wishing that he were dead (1 Kings 19:3–4). He was suffering from spiritual burn-out!

Have you ever felt like Elijah? Perhaps you are feeling like that right now. If so, what do you think has led you to that point?

> *'It is one thing to be tired in God's work, but quite another to be tired of God's work.'*

Look at the way God deals with Elijah in verses 5–9. Do you notice anything unusual? God doesn't lecture him on his faithlessness, or tell him to pull himself together and get on with his job. But what he does do is to allow him to rest. You see, God is far more interested in the worker, than he is in the work. Elijah was of more value to God than was the ministry he was doing. This is shown in the way that the Lord doesn't bypass Elijah, leaving him a burned-out shell of a man. He wants to restore him.

> *'God is more interested in the worker than the work'*

God knew that Elijah's first need was a physical one. It was only once Elijah had rested physically that the Lord moved on to his spiritual need. Many people try to find a spiritual solution to a physical problem, when what they actually need is a good holiday in order to recharge their batteries. Physical tiredness does affect our spiritual life, when we are too exhausted to pray, or too mentally stressed to read; that is why it is important to have a day of rest. God wants our bodies to catch up with our souls.

PRAY

Thank the Lord that, unlike the world's love, his love for you is not based on how successful you are but on whose you are. You may like to use the words of this hymn as your prayer:

> Just as I am, without one plea
> but that you died to set me free,
> and at your bidding 'Come to me!'
> O Lamb of God, I come.
>
> Just as I am, without delay
> your call of mercy I obey –
> your blood can wash my sins away:
> O Lamb of God, I come.
>
> Just as I am, though tossed about
> with many a conflict, many a doubt,
> fightings within and fears without,
> O Lamb of God, I come.

Just as I am, poor, wretched, blind!
Sight, riches, healing of the mind –
all that I need, in you to find:
O Lamb of God, I come.

Just as I am! You will receive,
will welcome, pardon, cleanse, relieve:
because your promise I believe,
O Lamb of God, I come.

Just as I am! Your love unknown
has broken every barrier down:
now to be yours, yes, yours alone,
O Lamb of God, I come.

Just as I am! Of that free love
the breadth, length, depth and height to prove,
here for a time and then above,
O Lamb of God, I come.

Charlotte Elliott, 1789–1871

Study 3 Back to Basics

PREPARE YOUR HEART

Meditate for a moment on these words of Jesus:

'If anyone would come after me, he must deny himself and take up his cross daily and follow me' (Lk 9:23).

Now reflect upon how these words impact your life when you substitute your own name for the word 'anyone'.

No longer mine, Lord, but yours,
Whate'er the fight, Lord, your cause,
Let me have all things, let me have naught,
Take every word, Lord, and every thought,
I gladly yield to your command,
No longer mine, no longer mine, but yours.

No longer mine, Lord, but yours,
To do with me as you desire,
To be exalted, or laid aside,
Take vain ambition and selfish pride.
Let me be humbled, you glorified,
No longer mine, no longer mine, but yours.

No longer mine, Lord, but yours,
The sovereign Lord who we adore.
We bow before you, our glorious King,
Our very lives, Lord, we freely bring.

A covenant human and divine,
No longer mine, no longer mine, but yours.

Geoff Baker, © 1988 Sovereign Lifestyle Music.

READ GOD'S WORD

Luke 9:18–27

In Roman occupied Israel at the time of Christ the symbol of the cross meant only one thing – death. Jesus was talking about the cost of commitment for those who wished to follow him: it meant denying their rights to their own lives and surrendering them willingly, totally, and freely to him. That, after all, is exactly what Christ did for us – he totally surrendered his life in order to spare us the punishment our sins deserve. Christ could request so much from those who wished to follow him on the basis of who he was. He was and is 'The Christ of God,' as Peter rightly acknowledged (Lk. 9:20).

It was C.T. Studd, the great cricketer and missionary pioneer in the latter part of the nineteenth century, who said: 'If Jesus Christ be God and gave himself for me, then no sacrifice can be too great for me to make for him.'

Whoever you are, however long you have been a Christian, humbly and openly examine your life right now and imagine Jesus speaking these words to you again: 'Who do you say that I am?' Is he the Christ who saved you years ago and was central to your life back then but has now been relegated to the edges of it? Or is he still the one to whom you bow the knee every morning as the Lord of your life?

Christ has never drifted in his commitment towards you, but perhaps you have drifted from your commitment towards him. If that is the case, come before him now, in fresh surrender giving the remainder of your life to him.

Further Reading: look up the following passages: Matthew 4:18–22; Romans 12;1,2.

> 'Every day that I wake up my first prayer is to die to my own selfish desires and to surrender my life afresh to Christ as my Lord and Saviour.'
> A missionary's daily prayer

PRAY

You may like to use the words which the Apostle Paul speaks in Philippians 3:7–14 as a basis for a prayer for your own life.

You may even like to use the words of this song as a prayer of dedication to the Lord

Breathe on me, breath of God:
Fill me with life anew,
That I may love what thou dost love,
And do what thou wouldst do.

Breathe on me, breath of God,
Until my heart is pure,
Until with thee I will one will,
To do and to endure.

Breathe on me, breath of God,
Till I am wholly thine,
Until this earthly part of me
Glows with thy fire divine.

Breathe on me, breath of God;
So shall I never die,
But live with thee the perfect life
Of thine eternity.

Edwin Hatch, 1835–1889

Study 4 Light in Times of Darkness

Begin by reading and reflecting on Psalm 23. Thank the Lord right now that he is your shepherd and as such will protect and provide for you as he has done in the past.

All the way my Saviour leads me:
What have I to ask beside?
Can I doubt his tender mercy,
Who through life has been my guide?
Heavenly peace, divinest comfort,
Here by faith in him to dwell!
For I know whate'er befall me,
Jesus doeth all things well.

All the way my Saviour leads me:
Cheers each winding path I tread;
Gives me grace for every trial,
Feeds me with the living bread.
Though my weary steps may falter,
And my soul athirst may be,
Gushing from the rock before me,
Lo! A spring of joy I see.

All the way my Saviour leads me:
O the fullness of his love!
Perfect rest to me is promised
In my Father's house above.

When my spirit, clothed, immortal,
Wings its flight to realms of day,
This my song through endless ages –
Jesus led me all the way.

Fanny J. Crosby, 1829–1915

READ GOD'S WORD

Psalm 27

This psalm was written by David during, or shortly after, a time of persecution. Perhaps it was when Saul was pursuing David, or it may have been when his own son Absalom rebelled against his father. One thing is certain: David knew that his security lay not in his own strength, for that would be limited, but in the Lord's, which was unlimited. The circumstances looked bleak at the natural level (vv. 1–3) but when he earnestly turned to the Lord he found hope in those dark times (vv. 4–6).

Have you ever felt that God has forgotten you or abandoned you?

Look again at verses 7–12. Here David pleads with the Lord not to ignore him in his moment of greatest need. Then in verse 10 David finds this incredible reassurance: 'Though my father and mother forsake me, the Lord will receive me.' David realized that even if his parents did forget about him, God could not. It was impossible for him to do so for he loved David too much. He is the perfect picture of all that parents truly ought to be toward their children. It was this reassurance that led David to pen the final verses of patient endurance in the face of adversity (see vv. 13,14).

Meditate: Write down on an index card one verse from this psalm which encourages you most, then look at that verse and meditate upon it throughout today.

> *'Can a mother forget the baby at her breast and have no compassion on the child she has borne? Though she may forget, I will not forget you!*
>
> *See, I have engraved you on the palms of my hands; your walls are ever before me.'*
> Isaiah 49:15,16

PRAY

Pray for any difficult circumstances that you are facing at this moment. What troubles you most about them? Tell God how you feel. Ask him for his perspective on them.

If God doesn't change the circumstances, what lessons might he be trying to teach you through them? What might he be trying to develop in you?

Ponder:
God is always at work, so, if he does not change your circumstances, he will change you to cope with your circumstances.

Further reading: 2 Corinthians 12:7–10

Study 5 What a Mighty God we Serve

PREPARE YOUR HEART

If it is possible, go outside and sit in the garden or a nearby park. Just for a moment, before you open your Bible, look around you at God's creation. Consider the variety of plants, trees, birds and insects. Observe the colours and textures in all their diversity. Look at the sky, the sun and the clouds.

Everything you see, no matter how large or small, is at this very moment totally reliant upon God's sustaining power to keep it alive and in its place (Heb. 1:3). That is amazing, isn't it? See how silently and effortlessly the Lord upholds everything, every second of every day and night.

Spend some time just praising him for his majesty and power.

READ'S GOD WORD

Psalm 19: 1–6
The psalmist may have sat for a moment just as you have done and marvelled at God's creation. He recognized that creation tells us that there is a God who made this universe and, more importantly, that he planned it down to the last detail. Incredible though it may seem, he made this world for you to enjoy, because as far as God is concerned you are the most important part of his creation.

Psalm 19:7–11

These verses show us that we matter so much to the Lord that he has provided instruction as to how we can enjoy a relationship with him. Read these verses again and just note how many benefits are obtained from reading his word. Perhaps you would like to underline them.

PRAY

Psalm 19:12–14

Notice how David turns from adoration (vv. 1–6) to instruction (vv. 7–11) which then leads him on to confession (vv. 12–14).

So often when we read God's word it is like switching a spotlight on our soul. The Lord highlights things in our lives which hinder us from fellowship with him. He does this not to condemn us but to discipline us so that we can see ourselves as we really are. He goes on to change us by his grace, mercy and help into what we ought to be. That is possible only when we confess our sin – both deliberate wrongs (v. 12) and hidden faults which we may be unaware of (v. 14).

The blood of Jesus has the power to cleanse us from every sin, to the extent that God can look upon us and accept us blameless and innocent (v. 13b)!

Come before the Lord now and confess any sin that you are aware of in your life. Ask the Lord to forgive you for sins that you had not been aware of. **Read 1 John 1:1–2:2 as an aid.**

Give thanks to the Lord for his immense mercy towards you. Ask the Lord that, by the power of the Holy Spirit, you may live for his glory today.

> 'When we look at the cross we see that God is so much more angry with us than we ever dared fear, but so much more loving than we ever dared hope!'

Study 6 The Freedom of Forgiveness

'There is a differerence between saying prayers and praying'

For many people the only time that they say the Lord's prayer is in church on a Sunday, and even then it is often a prayer 'spoken' rather than earnestly 'prayed' from the heart. With this in mind, I should like you slowly and considerately to pray through the Lord's prayer verse by verse. Having done this, move on to ponder upon these words from Psalm 32.

'Blessed is he whose transgressions are forgiven, whose sins are covered. Blessed is the man whose sin the Lord does not count against him and in whose spirit is no deceit' Psalm 32:1,2.

Now re-read these verses, putting your own name in place of the word 'he' or 'the man'. It sounds reassuring, doesn't it? If you have truly asked the Lord to forgive you for your sin, then it is absolutely true! You have God's word for it!

READ GOD'S WORD

Matthew 5:23,24
When I first became a Christian, the pastor of the church I attended invited a group of new converts

round to his home. It was a cold November night and we huddled round the open fire. He passed round a piece of paper and a pen and asked us to write down the things that we most regretted doing in our lives. Once we had finished writing he asked us to fold up the paper and place it into a paper cup. Nervously we all released our paper confessions wondering (and worrying) what he might do with them. He tossed the scraps of paper around in the cup with his finger, making us all fear what he was going to do next. After a long silence he said, 'This is exactly what happened to your sin when you put your trust in Jesus' sacrificial death on the cross,' and with that he threw the paper cup into the open fire! Needless to say we all breathed a sigh of relief; our individual shame and embarrassment had gone, and it felt so good!

> *'It is misleading to say that time heals – only forgiveness does that!'*
> Jim Graham

The truth of God's forgiveness hit home that November night. My sin was no longer remembered in the mind of God. He chose to forget it. What is more, so completely did he forgive me that he views me as spotless, like one without sin. Because of this I could know God as my Heavenly Father, and enjoy fellowship with him. How incredible! That night I inwardly sang my heart out to the Lord, thanking him for his mercy and love toward me.

PRAY

You know, the most liberating thing in the world is forgiveness. The beauty of it is that it liberates you as well as the person who has caused you wrong; for as long as you hold a grudge against someone you yourself will remain spiritually impoverished and out of fellowship with the Lord. We are instructed to forgive others just as in Christ Jesus God forgave us (see Eph. 4:30–32).

Perhaps there are people who you need to 'release' from captivity. They may have caused you great harm and upset you terribly, but being bitter towards them will do you no good; indeed it will affect your own relationship with the Lord. So why not release your offenders and pray the Lord's blessing on them? To pray in such a way would be a sign that you have forgiven them.

Recommended Books

The Bible – Essential!

devotional life

Buchanan, Alex, 1987, *Bible Meditation*, Kingsway
Dunn, Ronald, 1992, *Don't Just Stand There . . . Pray Something!*, Scripture Press
Eyre, Stephen, 1995, *Time With God*, IVP
Hybels, Bill, 1988, *Too Busy Not to Pray*, IVP
Kelly, Douglas F., *If God Already Knows Why Pray?*, Christian Focus Publications
McDonald, Gordon, 1987, *Ordering Your Private World*, Highland Books

Bible aids

Peterson, Eugene, 1995, *The Message – the New Testament paraphrased*, Navpress
Topical Memory System – *cards with key verses to memorize*, Navpress

Stibbs Alan (ed.), *Search the Scriptures*, IVP
Life Builder series, Scripture Union
Life Change series, Navpress
Christian Character Bible studies, IVP
Platt, Christine, *31 Days with Jesus*, Navigators
Blacklock, Brian, *What's in the Vineyard Today Lord?*, Navigators

daily Bible study notes

Alive to God, Scripture Union
Explore Bible notes for adults. St Matthias Press
Our Daily Bread, RBC Ministries USA
Hughes, Selwyn, *Every Day With Jesus*, Waverley

short daily devotionals

Chambers, Oswald, 1989, *My Utmost for His Highest*, Nova Publishing
Spurgeon, C.H., 1996, *Cheque Book of the Bank of Faith*
Spurgeon, C.H., *Morning & Evening*
Daily Light, Hodder & Stoughton

Bibliography

Baker, Howard, in *Christianity* October 1997

Bonar, Andrew, 1978, *Memoir and Remains of R.M. McCheyne*, Banner of Truth

The Concise Oxford Dictionary, 1990, OUP

Eyre, Stephen, *Time with God*, IVP

Steer, Roger, 1985, *George Müller's Experience of God*, Hodder & Stoughton

Wiersbe, Warren, 1994, *God Isn't in a Hurry*, Crossway

Becoming a Contagious Christian
How to Invest Your Life in Reaching Other People
Bill Hybels & Mark Mittelberg

Becoming a Contagious Christian is a proven plan for impacting
the spiritual lives of friends, family members, co-workers and
others. The material flows out of the real-life experience of Bill
Hybels, one of the foremost experts on reaching irreligious
people with the Gospel, and of Mark Mittelberg, Willow Creek's
evangeism trainer.

Powerful stories and teaching will help readers:

- Gain hope that their friends' lives can change.
- Be freed from the misconceptions of evangelism.
- Take steps to develop a 'contagious' character.
- Discover a natural approach to communicating their faith.
- Maximise opportunities to build relationships.
- Learn to articulate biblical truths in plain language.

Bill Hybels is senior pastor of Willow Creek Community Church
in South Barrington, Illinois. Willow Creek is the best attended
church in North America and is known for its outreach to
unbelievers in the Chicago area. Bill is the author of numerous
books, including *Tender Love, Laws of the Heart, Too Busy to
Pray* and *Fit to be Tied*, which he authored with his wife, Lynne.

Mark Mittelberg is Evangelism trainer for Willow Creek
Community Church and the Associate Director of Willow Creek
Association. He is also the primary author of the *Contagious
Christian Course*, a curriculum designed to help churches train
their people in relation evangelism.

ISBN 1-898938-60-1

alpha

The Pursuit of God
Daily Devotional
A.W. Tozer

"Happy is the Christian who reads a Tozer book when his soul is parched and God seems far away."
Warren Wiersbe

Tozer described *The Pursuit of God* as "a modest attempt to aid God's hungry children so to find Him." Since its first publication in 1948 thousands of people throughout the world have found spiritual refreshment in the pages of his classic work. Today over a million copies are now in print.

In this volume the complete text of *The Pursuit of God* has been divided into 31 daily meditation, allowing the reader to reflect on and absorb each portion. Quotations from some of Tozer's additional works and from other contemporary and classic authors further enhance the text.

A.W. Tozer has been described as 'a twentieth century prophet'. For 31 years he was Pastor of Southside Alliance Church in Chicago. He is author of over 40 books.

Edythe Draper is the author of *Draper's Book of Quotations*. Whilst working at Tyndale House Publishers she developed a series of devotional books for various ages.

ISBN 1-85078-278-4

OM
publishing

Discipline: The Glad Surrender
Elisabeth Elliot

Through personal anecdotes and biblical illustrations, Elisabeth Elliot reveals the fulfilment experienced by those who trust and obey God. She explores how we can discipline our minds, bodies, possessions, time and feelings by letting Christ have control of all areas of our lives. By doing so we can draw closer to God's will.

"From her opening remarks to the final words of triumph, Elliot guides the reader with love and firmness, with understanding and perception, and with reality and challenge."
Royal Service

Elisabeth Elliot is a lecturer, teacher and best-selling author. Her numerous books include *A Path Through Suffering, On Asking God Why* **and** *Keep a Quiet Heart.*

ISBN 1-85078-302-0

OM
publishing